CHECK FOR
PRICE GUIDE
BACK COVER

 W9-AXA-780

Fenton Glass
The 1980s Decade

MIDLOTHIAN
PUBLIC LIBRARY

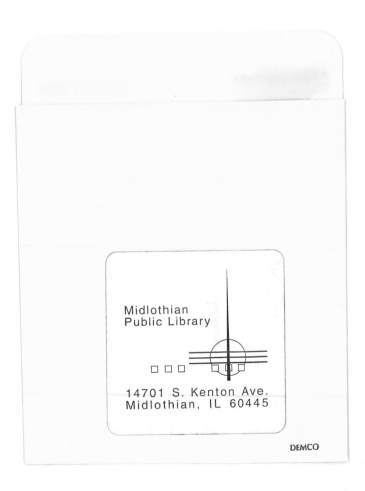

PB ISBN #1-57080-019-7   HB ISBN #1-57080-020-0

CONTENTS

FOREWORD

"Is there a Fenton glass book 4 yet?" someone said. I can't recall who asked, but the inquiry struck a chord. When the question was put to Frank Fenton and Dave Richardson, they responded with enthusiasm, and this book was begun. Each of the previous Fenton books had covered a twenty-five year period, but none of us could wait until the year 2005 arrived—too much had happened during the decade of the 1980s!

After Bill Heacock's death in 1988, I had helped Frank with the final editing of the third Fenton book, so I knew how interesting it would be to pore over the Fenton catalogues with Frank and to plan the glass photography with Dave. However, I also realized that I'd have to sort out the details of the Fenton history, since Dr. Eugene Murdock had passed away in 1992.

The task was initially daunting, but I was allowed to dig through files and records of all kinds. I was also privi-leged to interview three generations of Fentons and many longtime company employees as well as retirees. Wherever I went in the factory and offices, I met cheerful, friendly folks who were willing to search their memories and to answer questions about themselves and their work.

As the photography was being done and the book was taking shape, I became increasingly impressed with the Fenton organization and its people. Glassmaking is an ancient art, and this remarkable American company has been able to maintain the mystery and romance of yesteryear while using contemporary, state-of-the-art methods to assure quality and efficiency.

James Measell
June, 1996

4

ACKNOWLEDGEMENTS

First and foremost, I must thank the Fentons—Bill, Christine, Don, Frank, George, Lynn, Mike, Nancy, Randy, Shelley, and Tom—for their help and support in making this book a reality. They willingly granted interviews about themselves and their work, and many of them later reviewed drafts (and re-drafts!) of the chapters you see here. They helped get the facts straight, and they offered many constructive suggestions and comments.

Many Fenton Art Glass Company employees and Fenton Gift Shop employees also contributed to this book. Tamra Armstrong coordinated the effort by routing memos and drafts of chapters to the right people and by arranging interviews and meetings. Pam Dick helped with all of the photo shoots, and she prepared the first drafts of captions for hundreds of the items shown in color. When a particular piece of glass was needed, Pam found it. When checking and double-checking had to be done, Pam and Ann Stull pitched in, especially when deadlines were tight.

Mary Berry and Ann Murtha searched their memories and their files for vital information. Bobbie Duty gave me a crash course in understanding Fenton's shipping records, and Tami Lane searched the computer and the card files for color codes and other data. Don Cunningham, Joyce Sims and Chris Benson helped track down special orders and solve related problems.

Howard Seufer loaned his voluminous photo files, and Marsha Mumaugh located photos of Fenton reps. Susan Bryant, Linda Everson and Kim Plauché answered questions about decorating. Linda Frazier and Richard Delaney explained sandcarving, and Richard located glassware in the factory's nooks and crannies. Stan Vanlandingham made sure that the financial and statistical information was accurate. Shawn Godfrey, Albert King, and Wayne King provided information.

Fenton rep Randy Weikel shared information about his firm and his longstanding relationship with Fenton. Whitney Smith, who is affiliated with QVC, provided background and insights into Fenton's earliest ventures with QVC.

When the time came for the photography work, Frank Fenton searched the plant's storage rooms and the Fenton Museum for the glass of the 1980s. Hundreds of pieces were located and made ready for photo shoots. Many other items were needed, however, and the following individuals loaned articles of glassware shown in this book: Kelly Barker, Duward Barcley, Mary Clapper, Ron and Pam Dick, Bill and Fran Ersham, Ben Fenton, Bill and Elinor Fenton, Christine Fenton, Don and Donna Fenton, Lynn Fenton, Tina Ferrell, Dorothy Gates, Kerri Griffith, Ike and Betty Hardman, Dan and Carol Huff, Charles and Joan Illk, Kathy Kennedy, Melvin Lampton, Ed and Shirley Lehew, Jay Marshall, Shirley Roddy McGregor, Willa Norman, Dave Richardson, Robert Richardson, Dale and Eileen Robinson, Howard and Mary Seufer, Mr. and Mrs. Earl Smith, Richard and Ruby Staats, Delmer Stowasser, Monica Stull, Tom and Ann Stull, and Peggy Wherry. The dealers at the Williamstown Antique Mall let me "borrow" whatever was needed for a photo shoot, sometimes at a moment's notice.

Ferill Jeane Rice wrote the chapter devoted to the Fenton Art Glass Collectors of America, and the club's listing of glass made for the FAGCA (compiled by "Betty, Arvin and Irene") was most helpful.

Mr. Robert Richardson of Richardson Printing Corporation facilitated access to the storage area where many of the Fenton Art Glass Company's print jobs were preserved. Lee Parent cheerfully helped me find and sort the materials needed.

Book designer Brady Peery prepared the layout and added some attractive flourishes to make this book complete. Tarez Samra Graban of The Glass Press/Antique Publications did the typesetting, prepared the Index and attended to countless other details—all with efficiency and good humor.

James Measell
June, 1996

PUBLISHER'S INTRODUCTION

Perhaps the greatest thing about living in a town the size of Marietta is the potential to develop strong relationships that live on from one generation to another. This has certainly been the case with my family and the Fentons.

My connection with the Fenton family began when my father bought the Owens Printing Company in 1944 and moved to Marietta. One of the first things he did with his new business was to go knocking on the doors of the various industries around Marietta. The Fenton Art Glass Company was a natural place for him to call since they were one of the big employers in the area.

On his first visit, he remembers meeting two older gentlemen, one of whom was introduced to him as "Mr. Fenton" (Frank L.) and the other of whom was introduced simply as "Bob"! Dad recalls that when he went into his sales pitch, Bob pointed to a filing cabinet on which was stacked an overflowing pile of papers and said, "What in heaven's name do we want to advertise for? We can't fill all the orders we have now!"

Even though he didn't sell them any printing to be used to market their glass, he did get an order for letterheads, and that was about all the printing he did for them until the sixties.

By that time, Richardson Printing had become good at producing color printing and was one of the few printing companies in Ohio to be able to photograph, separate and print color all at one location. This combination of factors and its proximity to the Fenton factory made our shop an ideal choice for their catalog production.

Throughout the sixties and seventies, we printed catalogs, sales sheets, promotional pieces and hang tags, and my father became good friends with Frank M. Fenton and Wilmer "Bill" Fenton, his brother. It was a testament to the respect they had for the relationship and for my father that the second plate in the Craftsman Series was "The Printer" (circa 1971).

In 1975 I became involved in the family printing business and as a consequence I, too, met Frank and Bill. Although I was aware of them before (Frank had once invited me to sing in his church choir), I really didn't get to know them well until I got involved in the production of their catalogs and, subsequently, this series of books.

As the seventies closed and the eighties opened, I kept crossing paths with the next generation. I remember taking pictures of a young, vibrant teenager named Shelley, who was vying for a Bicentennial Queen title in 1976. On more than one occasion, I played tennis against Tom Fenton or George Fenton, both of whom are very good. Although Don Fenton is much too good for me to play against, I nonetheless met and talked to him many times on the golf course.

And the eighties, the decade covered in this volume, has been a great continuation of the relationship between the Fentons and the Richardsons. It is amusing to me that as my children age and compete in community athletics, they cross paths with the fourth generation of Fentons. One hopes that this generation will someday come to have the same warm feelings and respect for each other that the previous generations now enjoy.

Will I—or one of my sons—one day write an introduction to a fifth volume on Fenton Glass, wherein we talk about the accomplishments of the fourth generation?

To be continued...

David E. Richardson, Publisher
June, 1996

6

"It was the best of times. It was the worst of times." Charles Dickens' words in *Tale of Two Cities* capture the history of the Fenton Art Glass Company between 1980 and 1990. A poor general economy and pressure from imported giftwares dominated the early years, and the mid-1980s saw Fenton marketing a diversity of giftware products as well as glassware. By 1989, Fenton had rebounded, emphasizing traditional designs in glass while adding innovative colors and distinctive decorations.

The decade was difficult for Fenton, but it was devastating for other American glassmaking firms. Several long-time competitors—Fostoria, Imperial and Westmoreland—shut down their furnaces and closed their doors during the 1980s. Among the hand glass plants, Fenton was "number one," but in a diminishing and increasingly threatened industry.

In a speech to Fenton glass collectors in 1992, George and Nancy Fenton dubbed the 1980s "Life After Milk Glass Hobnail." Having experienced a "roller coaster ride of epic proportions," they reflected that Fenton's survival had been a serious concern. The company sought to maintain its sales volume with new ventures and directions—Katja, American Legacy, Artisan, Spotlight, Fenton-From-Afar, Gracious Touch, Christine Victoria, Bradford plates, Birthstone Bears, and anniversary and sentiment pieces as well as sandcarved special products and work for Avon, Princess House and Tiara. George summed it up: "Some succeeded, some worked for a while then disappeared, some bombed."

At the outset of the decade, Fenton set new sales records. Sales in 1979 were the highest ever, and net profits before taxes were second only to 1975. Sales set new records again in both 1980 and 1981. Although profits were down slightly, there was reason for optimism, particularly if the generally anticipated improvements in the national economy were to take place. However, the next several years brought a recession, and Fenton felt its effects. Net sales for 1982 dropped 20%, and the company showed a loss. Production costs were high, despite initiatives for efficiency. Conservation measures controlled fuel consumption, but the price of fuel had increased.

It got worse. The report from the Annual Stockholders Meeting held early in 1984 notes tersely: "1983 was not a good year." Indeed, it was not. Sales were off just 5.3%, but the company again showed an overall loss, this time in six figures. Fenton had not raised the prices on items in its line, and, although American consumers were spending more dollars for giftware, competition was keen, especially from imported gift items. The company decided to produce more articles to retail under $20.00 "in order to recapture lost customers."

Fenton did not sit still. New glass colors were developed, and additional shapes were introduced. Designers worked on new concepts. All sought to answer the question "What will sell?" The line for 1982 had about 200 new pieces, and the line for 1983 had approximately 300 new items. Yale and Frances Forman collaborated with Fenton on An American Legacy, a Federal-style ware marketed to department stores and finer gift stores. A contemporary-style line developed by Swedish designer Katja was introduced. Although the Katja pieces also opened some department store doors to the Fenton line, they proved both difficult to make and slow to sell in the marketplace.

About 1985, following the advice of Don Meckstroth of Trundle Associates and the Richardson/Smith consulting firm, the company adopted a new marketing strategy. Fenton glassware products were segmented into three groups—Artisan (upscale, higher price); Classic (traditional ware sold by independent gift shops); and Spotlight (lower-priced glassware for large volume outlets).

Private mould work (particularly for customers such as Avon and Princess House) generated extra sales dollars. Manufacturing innovations allowed the company to operate more effectively. A new rotary press was operated successfully (especially on glass animal figurines), and pad printing equipment helped with the production of low-cost decorated ware. A new continuous tank was available for crystal glass. Attrition and layoffs reduced the ranks of employees, both salaried and union.

In the mid-1980s, Fenton diversified its involvement within the giftware business by introducing Fenton-From-Afar and by the acquisition of Thee Bakers Dozen, a California-based manufacturer which was renamed Christine Victoria. At the meeting of stockholders in early 1986, new President George Fenton put it this way: "Our corporate strategy is to change from a manufacturer of handmade glassware to a supplier of a complete line of giftware." A home party plan, called Gracious Touch, was developed to sell Fenton glass, Fenton-From-Afar and Christine Victoria. In glassware, many Fenton limited editions, including the Connoisseur Collection, were launched. A December national sales meeting, bringing Fenton reps from across the nation to Williamstown, strengthened the sales organization.

By the late 1980s, Fenton's glass business had regained its strength among the company's traditional gift shop customers and within department store accounts. A new marketing opportunity presented itself through the magic of television in the form of a shop-from-home concept called QVC, and Chairman of the Board Bill Fenton and his daughter Shelley worked closely with this account. Fenton also acquired significant "special market" customers for glassware. A weakened U. S. dollar helped Fenton compete with imported giftwares. On the negative side, Christine Victoria had faltered (despite new management and relocation to nearby Vienna), and both Fenton-From-Afar and Gracious Touch were on the verge of being discontinued.

The "back to basics" theme begun in 1986-87 enabled the company to rededicate itself to producing handmade glass in traditional shapes and colors. This focus gradually took hold, and the company's emphasis on Fenton glass collectibles increased. Several Fenton colors, particularly Dusty Rose and Country Cranberry, enjoyed long periods of popularity and strong sales. At a Board meeting in 1990, President George Fenton said that "business for the glass company has been good," and he noted that "our biggest problem is an inability to make as much glass as we can sell." The Fenton Art Glass Company had survived a difficult decade and emerged from it with optimism.

The chapters which follow trace the changes and developments in both Fenton's people and its products throughout the 1980s. The Fenton family—management, employees and reps—is discussed next, and the Fenton line—colors, shapes and treatments—occupies Chapter Eighteen. Other elements of the Fenton story, ranging from collectible glass (such as the Connoisseur Collection and items for Mother's Day and Christmas) and special products to Fenton's diversification ventures, are the focus of separate chapters later.

Chapter Seventeen
THE FENTON FAMILY:
CONTINUITY AND CHANGE

The Fenton "family" really includes three separate but closely related groups—Fenton management, Fenton employees and Fenton reps. Overall policy and direction are determined by Fenton management, while Fenton employees produce the product and Fenton reps take it to the marketplace. Together, they are a remarkable team and a close "family" in the best sense of the word.

Fenton Management

Upon the deaths of Frank L. Fenton and Robert C. Fenton in 1948, the responsibility for running the Fenton Art Glass Company was vested in the "second generation," Frank M. Fenton and Wilmer C. "Bill" Fenton. As President and Vice-President, respectively, the brothers worked well together, but they had somewhat different interests. Bill relished the marketing and sales side of the business, and Frank enjoyed working with design concepts and solving manufacturing problems. As one current Fenton employee remarked, "Frank made it and Bill sold it!"

Between 1965 and 1982, most of Frank and Elizabeth Fenton's children (Tom, Mike and George) and all of Bill and Elinor Fenton's (Don, Randy, Shelley and Christine) joined the Fenton team. All had worked part-time at the company during their high school or college years. In the mid-1980s, this "third generation" of Fentons assumed most of the key executive and managerial positions at Fenton.

In 1978, Frank decided to relinquish the President's post. At the time, his wife Elizabeth was ill with amyotropic lateral sclerosis (Lou Gehrig's disease), the affliction which took her life in September, 1980. Understandably, Frank wanted to spend as much time as possible with her at their home. Frank and Bill began to talk about other changes and the various possibilities for succession within the company's executive positions.

When Frank stepped down as President, Fenton's Directors created a new position, Chairman of the Board. Previously, the company's President had presided at the Board's meetings. Bill Fenton became President in 1978, and he and Frank often talked about the company's long-term picture, sometimes inviting other family members into these discussions. Ultimately, George Fenton succeeded Bill as President. Tom Fenton recalls that "it was a smooth transition, and George took control in a very constructive way."

George Fenton had been full-time with the company since 1972, the year after his graduation from Wesleyan University, where he studied physics and astronomy. His first full-time position was as "assistant to the President" (which meant that he worked on whatever project Frank had in mind for him!). Later, George was involved with inventory control in the Shipping Deparment, and he became foreman of the Decorating Department in 1976. At that time, Fenton was implementing wage incentive programs for the decorators which were similar to those in place for Hot Metal workers. George had worked on the development of these incentives, and he found it ironic that he was to supervise the

decorators right at the inception of the plan.

From 1979-85, George was manager of manufacturing and represented the company in labor negotiations with the American Flint Glass Workers Union. He had developed a real appreciation for the conditions and problems encountered in Hot Metal while working on blow shop production problems, and he had been involved with labor-management problem-solving committees. During contract talks with the AFGWU locals in 1982 and 1985, George spoke for the company in meetings with the union's representatives.

In 1985, the lines of succession became clear when George was appointed Executive Vice-President by the Board of Directors. There was no surprise when, a year later, he became President. Frank stepped down as Chairman of the Board, and Bill went from the Presidency to Chairman of the Board. A decade later, with a smile, George likened his move to "riding in an airplane plummeting toward the ground and being asked to take over as pilot," an analogy he also recalls invoking at the time. Frank suggests a different comparison: "Although the airplane was off course and losing altitude, there was adequate fuel in the reserve tanks. The new pilot was being asked to take over at a time when other planes were crashing all around."

Although Frank held no formally-designated position, his activities in the 1980s were far from the usual connotations of "retired." Relocated to an office "just down the hall although a lot smaller than the one I used to enjoy," he went to the factory almost daily to look after projects ranging from the Fenton Museum to special souvenirs for glass collectors' clubs. He continued as an active participant on the design committee and, subsequently, the new product development committee.

Many letters from collectors with questions about Fenton glass or antique glass came to Frank's desk. With patience (and considerable tolerance for the rather basic inquiries), he answered them, often spending hours with old Fenton inventory records or catalogs and price lists before dictating a letter. He looked forward to attending the conventions of various Carnival glass clubs, especially that of the Heart of America Carnival Glass Association, which meets each April in Lenexa, Kansas.

As President and, later, Chairman of the Board, Bill Fenton continued to be active in the sales side at Fenton, working closely with his eldest son, Don. With pride and affection, Bill speaks of "grooming" Don to take over as national sales manager, even to the point of telling assistant Tom Lubbers when he hired him that Tom should not look forward to a promotion, because the position was earmarked for Don. Almost weekly in the 1980s, letters to Fenton's reps went out over either Bill's or Don's signature. Bill also went to the glass and giftware shows, and he was involved with marketing and sales decisions as well as the design committee and the new product development committee.

In the late 1980s, Bill was the key figure in Fenton's deepening relationship with the QVC home shopping channel. He recalls a young QVC production assistant asking if he was nervous as she attached a microphone

Front row: **Lynn E. Fenton, Sales & Marketing Specialist; Christine L. Fenton, Data Processor, Fenton Gift Shop; Shelley Fenton-Ash, Graphics Manager & Key Accounts; Nancy G. Fenton, Director of Design.** Center: **Wilmer C. "Bill" Fenton, Chairman of the Board; Frank M. Fenton, Historian.** Back row: **Don A. Fenton, Vice-President of Sales; George W. Fenton, President; Michael D. Fenton, Purchasing Manager & Safety Director; Thomas K. Fenton, Vice-President of Manufacturing; Randall R. Fenton, Treasurer, Fenton Gift Shop.**

to his lapel just before his first show. "No," he replied, "*should* I be nervous?" He was at ease and natural, and his appearances—whether on camera or by telephone—soon became a vital part of the show.

On QVC broadcasts, Bill often invited viewers to "come down and see us in West Virginia." And they did! More than a few Fenton Gift Shop visitors spotted Bill and came forward to say "hello," introduce themselves and chat about seeing him on QVC with Fenton glass. Other fans went to the office reception area and asked for Bill so that they could have snapshots taken with him. "What I'm doing on the show is just being myself," Bill says, a bit bemused but nonetheless flattered by his celebrity status.

As Vice-President of Manufacturing and Plant Manager, Tom Fenton presided over numerous changes and innovations. These ranged from fuel and energy conservation programs, which helped Fenton hold the line on costs, to the installation of a new continuous tank for crystal glass and the purchase of equipment for sandblasting or decorating by pad printing. In the early 1980s, Tom chaired the Industrial Advisory Committee of the Society for Glass Science and Practices. This group spearheaded a comprehensive study of the U. S. hand glass industry in 1981-82 by Trundle Consultants, Inc.

"We took the Trundle report very seriously," Tom remembers. "It helped us focus on trends in both manufacturing and marketing." As a result, he concentrated on improving Fenton's product planning and scheduling

practices for several years and then gradually pulled back into the manufacturing sphere. In the late 1980s, Tom was responsible for the company's CIQ program (Continuous Improvement in Quality), and a dozen managers and supervisors from all areas of the plant reported to him.

A 1964 graduate of Ohio Wesleyan University, Tom did graduate work at Ohio University in nearby Athens. Tom and his wife Sharon have two daughters, Jamie and Jennifer, and a son, Scott.

Just outside Mike Fenton's office, a sign records the company's cumulative work days "without an accident." As Safety Director since 1985, his philosophy is to "keep well ahead" of increasingly strict industrial practices and government regulations rather than waiting to react to mandated changes. The company's excellent safety record and high marks on OSHA inspections are a source of pride.

Mike attended Wooster College and served in the United States Navy for about four years, including two Pacific tours of duty during the Vietnam era. Mike and his wife Kathy have two daughters—Meredith and Natalie—and Mike has a daughter, Kerry, from a previous marriage.

As Fenton's Purchasing Manager since 1973, Mike is responsible for assuring a ready supply of the raw materials for glassmaking, but his greatest challenges lie in finding suitable vendors for a myriad of other necessities—lamp parts, vinyl masks for sandcarving, special

10

glues and decorating materials as well as packing and shipping supplies of all kinds. When Fenton was developing its 8600 clock, for example, Mike investigated foreign and domestic sources for proper works to fit properly and perform reliably.

During high school and college, Don Fenton worked in the Fenton Gift Shop as well as the Shipping Department and, later, in sales. He was graduated from Muskingum College with a B. S. in mathematics and captained the golf team (he remains an avid golfer today with a seven handicap). Don especially remembers the encouragement of Ruth Holzapfel in Fenton's order entry department, and he also recalls the help of his predecessor, Tom Lubbers, who was then selling Fenton with Alan Symmes in New England.

Don was appointed Assistant Sales Manager in 1975, and he became Sales Manager in 1978, when his father Bill succeeded Frank as President. From the mid-1970s through the early 1980s, Don developed most of Fenton's catalogs, and Dr. Robert Fischer, Fenton's Director of Personnel Research, wrote much of the copy. In 1985, Don became Vice-President—Sales. Don and his wife Donna have three children: Greer, Craig and Brice.

Don travels frequently to regional and national giftware shows and is in frequent contact with the company's representatives, through regular letters and scheduled meetings at gift shows or in Williamstown. In the 1980s, he worked with sales efforts for the entire Fenton line—glassware, Christine Victoria and Fenton-From-Afar. "We were searching hard for the right combinations," he recalled, "but glass was always our bread and butter." After Fenton was "trying anything and everything" for a few years in the mid-1980s, the company settled on the Back to Basics theme. In reflection, Don sees this as an emphasis on "doing what we know how to do best" and credits "listening to our reps and customers" as underscoring this decision.

Nancy Gollinger Fenton, who is married to George, graduated from Williamstown High School and Denison University. They have two sons, Ben and David.

Nancy was doing post-graduate work in marketing through Ohio University classes which met at Marietta College when Tom Fenton recruited students for part-time work at Fenton. She began by perusing trade publications and writing summaries of trends in the giftware marketplace. Nancy moved into Fenton's sales department in 1982 when she became involved in the company's projects with Yale and Frances Forman's American Legacy and the Swedish designer Katja (see Chapter Nineteen).

Nancy was appointed Manager of New Product Development in 1985. She developed many of the groupings of Fenton glass and Christine Victoria products later in the 1980s, and she particularly recalls the "BIG splash" at Macy's in New York during 1986 when the department store's center giftware display featured Fenton's Dusty Rose glass with coordinated Christine Victoria items. Now, a decade later, she provides overall direction for Fenton's design decisions. An active participant in national color and design conferences, she also seeks inspiration from customers and collectors as well as old glass at antique shows or pictured in books.

Shelley Fenton (now Shelley Fenton Ash) was a tour guide and spent a summer in Fenton's order department during her college years. After graduating with a marketing degree from West Virginia University in 1982, she went full-time with the company in sales and also worked with some special order customers before assuming responsibility for all Fenton catalogues and other printed materials. She was appointed Assistant Sales Manager in 1985 and traveled to many regional and national giftware shows until 1992.

When Fenton first became associated with QVC in 1987, Shelley and Bill worked closely with QVC executives to develop the first Fenton items offered through this avenue. This sales area grew rapidly, and QVC is now among Fenton's most significant customers. Shelley continues to develop new items for QVC.

After the birth of a child in 1993, Shelley reduced her work schedule somewhat, but she continues to be responsible for Fenton catalogs and other sales materials via desktop publishing, and she remains an active participant in design and sales decisions. Shelly and her husband Daniel have a daughter, Amanda, and a son, Alex.

Randy Fenton was employed in the Gift Shop during his school years, and he worked with his brother Don in sales after graduating from Marietta College with a business management major in 1975. He went back to the Gift Shop in 1984 and is now Treasurer of that organization. Randy and his wife Debbie have three children—Danielle, Cassy, and Justin.

Incidentally, the Fenton Gift Shop and the glass company are separate corporations, and the Gift Shop buys glassware just like any other Fenton customer, although, as Randy noted, "shipping and re-stocking are easy."

During the 1980s, the Gift Shop began its annual February sales. These grew from simple clearance/discount sales to move discontinued items and other inventory into real bonanzas for the eager Fenton glass enthusiasts who were excited over the collectible glass from the line as well as the experimental pieces, samples and other "one-of-a-kind" items offered for sale during the mid- and late 1980s. "We expanded the modular displays ceilingward to offer about twice as much merchandise—Fenton glass as well as other items," Randy recalled, "and Jack Neilson really helped us with the non-Fenton collectibles." In 1989, the Fenton Gift Shop began to offer special pieces of Fenton glass as part of its February sale. The first group consisted of items made in "Almost Heaven" Blue Slag.

Christine Fenton worked part-time in the Gift Shop and as a tour guide during high school and college, but she spent seven years as an employee at Union Carbide before going full-time in the Fenton Gift Shop. In 1980, Christine moved to customer service for the glass company, and she recalls the sometimes hectic transition from processing mail orders to a toll-free 800-number for Fenton accounts: "We just got busier and busier!"

Now back with the Fenton Gift Shop in data processing, Christine has her own favorite pieces of Fenton glass—tobacco jars and the Rosalene color. She has several pieces made by Fenton for Levay, but her top choice is the Chessie Cat covered jar in Rosalene.

The first member of the "fourth generation" to join Fenton was Lynn Fenton, the daughter of Frank Fenton's eldest son, Frank, who has a career in animal husbandry. As a youngster, Lynn resided in Venezuela, but she lived in Williamstown with George and Nancy throughout her high school and college years and was a tour guide during the summers. After graduation from Bowling Green State University, she went on to the American Graduate School of International Management in Phoenix for work in international finance.

Before coming "back home" to Fenton as Sales and Marketing Specialist in 1994, Lynn was employed by EDS for about seven years. Working out of Dallas, London or Detroit, she traveled frequently as a member of an EDS manufacturing consulting group. "I was always thinking about how my work at EDS could be used in this factory," Lynn said. In 1996, she was involved with starting the Fenton *Glass Messenger* newsletter.

Stan Vanlandingham was a constant as management and executive changes took place in the 1980s. Stan earned his B. S. in Economics from Ohio State and began

Stan Vanlandingham

work as a financial analyst. By 1974, he was Controller of Sperry-Rand's Marietta Operations (now Kardex). When Sperry-Rand wanted Stan to transfer to Michigan, he and his family decided not to move, and he became Controller at Fenton in 1976. Don Alexander was then considering retirement, and Stan's responsibilities quickly increased. In 1978, he became Fenton's Secretary and Assistant Treasurer, and, in 1983, he was elected Secretary/Treasurer and Chief Financial Officer. Stan and his wife Ruth have two children, Stan and Megan.

One might wonder why a non-Fenton occupies this position. Stan provides his own answer, underscoring the advantages of "outside" expertise in the areas of finance, planning and controls. Stan examined Fenton's cash management practices, and concerted efforts were made to maximize income by investing cash balances on a daily basis in higher yield government securities. As a result, income from interest increased, and the company has continued to invest in this way.

When financing was needed in the 1980s, Stan helped obtain adequate lines of credit at favorable interest rates. As the new Fenton management team began to take hold, Stan helped design and implement the new management controls they desired. Drawing on the concepts of an outside consultant in cost reduction, these systems set objectives and provide accountability at every level of the organization over time (hourly, daily, weekly, etc.) by mandating that monitoring take place and solutions (or readjustments in objectives) be implemented. This practice of goal-setting, monitoring and action-implementation is currently being extended to Strategic Planning for long-term performance improvement in all aspects of Fenton's business.

Fenton Employees

In its broadest context, the phrase "Fenton family" goes well beyond those who bear the name or hold executive positions in the company. The strong work ethic and sense of shared responsibility extends throughout the employees at the Williamstown plant and to the sales representatives across the nation and around the world.

Glassmaking is an extraordinarily complex process, and the casual visitor on a Fenton tour really sees just a fraction of the total workforce. Every piece of glass is touched, directly or indirectly, by dozens of pairs of hands, ranging from those who design the articles and prepare the batch to those in Hot Metal and Cold Metal who make it and the people in support areas who see that it's properly packed, shipped on time and, eventually, paid for!

During the 1980s, Joe Voso, Jr., Fenton's labor-management specialist, started an informal company publication. After several years of mimeographed issues (modestly titled simply NEWSLETTER), the publication was printed under the banner *The Fenton World* for a time. Reflecting Joe's personal optimism and caring spirit, these monthly newsletters combined news and suggestions with important product quality and plant safety issues.

The newsletters listed the sons and daughters who were graduating from high school or college, and they also conveyed information about blood donor drives, Community Chest and United Way campaigns, or services available to employees. By October, 1981, Fenton had in place a comprehensive employee assistance program which offered personal counseling, help with finances, and medical services such as blood pressure checks and hearing and vision tests.

When longtime glassworkers Theodore Vincent and Pete Dallison retired, they were spotlighted in brief articles. Employees returning from lay-offs were welcomed back, and a genuine feeling of teamwork and camaraderie is evident. Workers who were off due to illness or injury were noted, and occasional voluntary collections ($1 per week from co-workers) were mentioned. "The money was nice to get," said one employee who had

Sonny Burdette (presser).

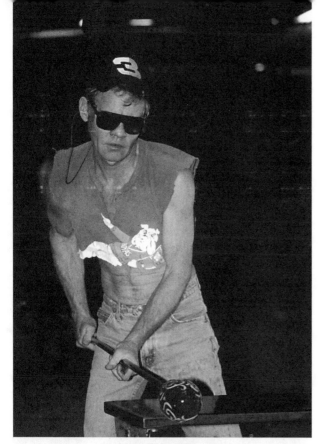

Dick Maidens (blower).

Blow shop glassworkers (from left): Ernie Phillips, Chuck Handel and Tod Uppole.

been off sick, "but knowing that people cared about me was a lot nicer."

Often, Joe's newsletters recognized workers who had made suggestions which conserved energy by installing switches, improved production by reducing losses or called attention to safety hazards such as the need for non-skid floor paint. The new sandcarving division was profiled, and the results of a labor-management meeting over the Trundle Report were detailed. The May, 1983, issue of *The Fenton World* emphasized quality standards and defect detection, announcing a factory-wide suggestion box contest. The result was a "Ware Care" program which established accountability controls department by department and created numerous changes in the handling of glassware in both Hot Metal and Cold Metal areas.

Many Fenton employees are represented by two local unions, No. 22 and No. 508, both affiliated with the American Flint Glass Workers Union. No. 22 enrolls the mouldmakers and the skilled glassworkers from Hot Metal, and No. 508 is composed of Cold Metal workers involved in other aspects of production, such as selecting, decorating, and packing.

New union contracts are negotiated about every three years, depending upon the length of the previous agreement. To the outsider, these contracts are veritable thickets of nearly impenetrable verbiage, filled with rules regarding everything from water breaks and vacation pay to seniority protection and specific regulations for production. This rule governs the operation of a glazer in Fenton's Hot Metal department: "Articles placed on a former to be glazed on edge and which are not changed from their original shape, but are kept on the former on which first placed in the hole until cold enough to carry into the lehr, or are not touched by anyone to restore the original shape may be done without a finisher, provided the presser and gatherer shall be paid lehr count for all ware except bad ware from their own fault." Even the definition of a piece of glassware can be tricky: "A Nappy, whose height is equal to or greater than $7/16$ of its diameter measurement, shall be called a Deep Nappy."

In 1979, contract bargaining bogged down over wages, and a ten-week strike resulted. During the 1980s, there were no strikes as negotiations took place in 1982, 1985, and 1989. The 1982 contract talks took place without the manufacturer's group in place, but Fenton avoided a strike, although some other plants (such as Imperial) had lengthy work stoppages. The fact that wages and benefits for bargaining unit employees constitute the largest single segment of product cost was emphasized often by the company in negotiations during the 1980s.

The financial hard times facing the company in 1985 resulted in a contract which froze wages for three years. At this time, the company was reducing prices on some glassware to stimulate sales. Employees were concerned about job security, since the number of Hot Metal shops had decreased 40% in four years and the total of hourly employees had been reduced by about 25%. In a statement at the outset of negotiations, George Fenton emphasized the company's needs for flexibility and cost reductions as well as an understanding of the workers' desire for job security. Prior to 1985, the skilled glassworkers represented by local union No. 22 had no seniority rights and could not "bump" back into jobs gov-

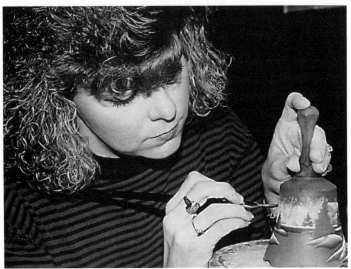

Jenni Cunningham (decorator).

erned by local union No. 508. Consequently, many good skilled workers who were laid off in the early 1980s never returned to Fenton. Ultimately, an agreement was reached which provided for both "plant seniority" and "department seniority" to the skilled workers in case they were not needed at skilled work.

By mutual consent in 1988, the three-year contract reached in 1985 was extended through 1989. This period was marked by the resumption of cooperative labor-management activities, including regular meetings among workers' groups and supervisors as well as the inauguration of the company's CIQ (Continuous Improvement of Quality) program. The contract reached in 1989 provided modest wage increases, although the company had not yet regained its former records of sales and profits.

In reflecting upon the changes in the 1980s, Frank Fenton observed that the dominance of milk glass Hobnail actually "made it easy" to keep in touch with the workforce during day-to-day operations in the 1960s and 70s. When problems developed, meetings between Frank and the other parties usually cleared the air and resolved disputes. As the glassmaking operation became increasingly complex in the 1980s, more batch melts were required and the introduction of new items and new treatments was the order of the day. The giftware marketplace also became more complex as customer needs and preferences began to drive product development. Fenton's management team, especially George and Tom, began to address these complexities through frequent labor-management meetings, encouraging employee participation and open communication.

Many Fenton employees and retirees are active in church groups, community and school affairs or various clubs and other organizations. Retired Fenton employees drop by the plant from time to time to renew acquaintances, and many attend the annual December luncheons. Although their working days at Fenton are behind them, they continue to express pride and satisfaction at their work. "It's a fine place," one man said. "You got a good day's pay for a good day's work, and you were side by side with good people from management right on down."

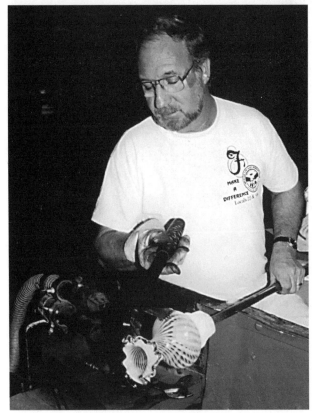

Dave Vincent (finisher).

Fenton Reps

Once the design decisions are implemented at the factory and the glassware is being made, Fenton's sales and marketing efforts quickly take shape, and the "reps" (manufacturers representatives) prepare to sell the glass to their accounts. Product launches occurred twice per year at the April and November New York City tabletop shows, and Fenton also developed regular promotions for Valentine's Day and Christmas.

Usually, major new product introductions took place in January; June marked the debut of Christmas items and limited editions. By the late 1980s, the Valentine's Day program (which then also included Easter items) began in September, and the Christmas promotions were launched in April. Fenton also mounted regular sales efforts for Milk Glass, and other special programs dealt with additions to a popular line (handpainted Strawberries on French Opalescent), the introduction of Regency in crystal, or an assortment of opalescent pitchers and cruets.

In the 1980s, Fenton's reps covered 49 states. Many reps maintained permanent showrooms for wholesale buyers, and all of Fenton's reps earn commissions on their sales. Each has a defined "territory" and travels to call on established accounts and to meet with potential new accounts as new gift shops are established and other opportunities present themselves. When Fenton has a new product, much of its market success depends upon the hard work and enthusiasm of the sales force to place it with as many accounts as possible.

The Fenton rep network has been remarkably stable over the years. Many of the names listed in the 1979-80 Fenton catalog appear in later catalogs during the decade,

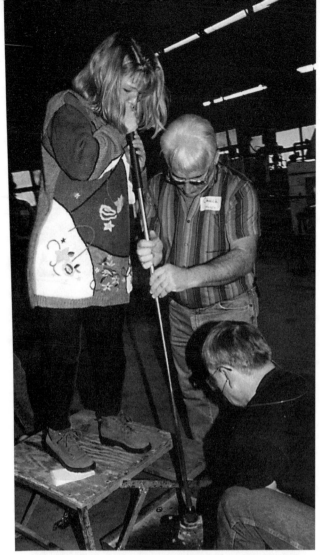

Rep Carol Belanger tries glassblowing with the help of glassworkers Chuck Handel (holding blowpipe) and Dave Emrick.

Glassworker Tom Ingram coaches rep Randy Weikel in a finishing operation.

and quite a few have affiliations with earlier reps. Robert Benson of Rochester, New York, for example, had worked with Carl Voigt, the rep who handled Fenton in upstate New York. When Voigt retired, Benson took over and maintained a successful record. The John H. Evans Company of Beaver Falls, Pa., began selling Fenton glass in 1955. Evans was instrumental in getting Fenton to add lamps to the line, and these often served as a focal point in displays of Fenton glass in gift shops. After he passed away, his wife Jane headed the organization for several years before selling it to salesmen Jim Allen and Fred Rathke, who continued the business under the Evans name.

When longtime Fenton rep Howard B. Aronow decided to retire in the mid-1980s, the company assumed the lease on his New York City location at 225 Fifth Avenue. Richardson/Smith redesigned the display areas, and the Fenton Corporate Showroom was established. In the late 1980s, The Moore Organization was retained to handle the sales territory in the New York City area as well as northern New Jersey.

For many years, Martin M. Simpson and Company represented Fenton in parts of the Midwest (Illinois, Indiana, Iowa, Michigan, Wisconsin) as well as Missouri, eastern Kansas and Nebraska. Ted Figler ran this organization in the 1970s and early 1980s; upon his retirement, several changes were made. Figler suggested that his longtime associate, Jack Walsh, become Fenton's rep in Michigan. The Simpson organization decided to discontinue working in Nebraska, Kansas and Missouri. Simpson's Roger Swiatek suggested that Maurice ("Mo") Childers and Associates cover this territory. Figler's niece, Barbara Ramberg, and his nephew, Dennis Figler, took over the Simpson organization and retained Illinois, Indiana and southern Wisconsin.

During the 1980s, there were a few major changes in Fenton's reps. The Texas area formerly handled by Thomas and Moore was assumed by Louise Lea Wright Company for several years and then by SMI Associates. When Scott Williams retired, he suggested that responsibility for the Northwest area (Washington and Oregon) be given to Dick Gibson and Associates. The Gibson group was subsequently honored as Fenton's "Organization of the Year" twice in succession.

The A. L. Randall Company of Chicago was Fenton's longtime rep to the florist trade, a market of some significance, as sales typically accounted for about 6% of Fenton's annual volume. After January 1, 1987, however, florists could place orders directly through Fenton's regular sales reps. Previously, they had not called on florists because of Fenton's ties with Randall. Fenton reps convinced Bill and Don that they could handle this business, and the conflicts arising when a new Randall florist account opened near an existing Fenton account could be avoided. For Fenton, "this was a tough decision but one that had to be made to fit our plans for the late '80s and '90s." During 1987, the company launched several promotional efforts to reach the "florist customer" with sales information about Fenton glass, Christine Victoria and Fenton-From-Afar items.

The MacLennan Sales Company of Los Angeles had had all of California (as well as Nevada and Arizona), but this territory was split up in the 1980s. Peddlers Too took over northern California and northern Nevada, while

Koch, Pruett and Associates became responsible for Arizona and New Mexico. The Flanagan Agency was hired to cover southern California and southern Nevada.

Overseas sales of Fenton glass have never been a particularly high percentage of sales volume (typically 1-2%), but the company has had successful relationships with reps in several foreign countries. Gregg Giftware looked after Fenton accounts in western Canada for a time, and W. J. Hughes and Sons held forth in the Toronto area before George Palliser Ltd. took over. In Australia, F. R. Barlow and Sons, Ltd., represented Fenton for quite some time until the early 1980s, but the company was sold and its successor, Jankie Consolidated Ltd., failed. R. H. Hall Proprietary Ltd. took over in 1987. During the 1980s, Fenton also had brief relationships with reps in England (La Reine Ltd.) and Japan (Hirota Glass Co. Ltd.).

In 1986, Fenton decided to convene a gathering of its reps in Williamstown in addition to the regular sales meeting held in conjunction with the New York City Tabletop show. These December sales meetings became an annual event, featuring awards for "Rep of the Year" and "Organization of the Year." A special sales award for the Decade of the '80s was presented to the Ivystone Group of Eagle, Pa., which was then responsible for eastern Pennsylvania and southern New Jersey. Today, Ivystone's territory also includes eastern Virginia, Delaware, Maryland and Washington D.C.

The annual meetings have served to increase the reps' identification with the company and to educate them about the Fenton product and the glassmaking process. The reps have also gained a greater appreciation of the skills of Fenton's employees. Reps often make suggestions about additions to the line or new products, and Fenton management listens very carefully to these.

Fenton rep Randy Weikel, whose family organization (The Weikels) has been selling Fenton glass in the Southeast for forty years, has been an enthusiastic participant in the sales meetings: "They're fun and great times for learning," he said. "The factory floor experience— actually trying to put a handle on a basket—really makes you more confident in talking about and selling hand-made glassware."

Each December session was built around a theme ("Professionalism," "Get Fit with Fenton," etc.), and the reps enjoyed being in the plant and having time to become familiar with new products and colors, to explore sales-related ideas and issues and to get to know each other better. "There's a great feeling of loyalty and family," Randy Weikel noted, "and it goes both ways— from the reps to the company and from the company to the reps."

✳ ✳ ✳ ✳ ✳ ✳

The glassmaking enterprise—from design and manufacturing to marketing and sales—is both interesting and complex. Each area must work well for the total effort to be successful. No area is immune from challenges and changes. One of Fenton's former competitors summed it up this way: "No one does it better than Fenton!"

Rep Janice Johnson and glassworker Ron Bayles work together.

Rep Barb Ramberg concentrates as she decorates a Christmas ornament.

In the giftware business, consumer trends emerge and today's fashions may fade and fall out of favor quickly. Fenton's customer—the independent retail store—continually asks "What's new? What's new?" and hopes the end consumer will be eager for these new styles and colors. Fenton catalogs from the 1980s reveal the broad changes in the line. The amount of milk glass diminished greatly, and opaque glass gave way to transparent colors. The number of color codes grew dramatically, with almost three times as many (97) available in 1992 compared to 1980 (35). Heavy patterns, including Hobnail, were replaced by pieces with clean lines. Special occasion pieces came to occupy a prominent place in the line.

How did it happen? Why did it happen? What were the conditions in the glass industry and the giftware trade that produced these changes? How did Fenton respond to the changes and the challenges? What new colors were developed? What new items were successful in the marketplace? The answers emerge when one looks at the decade of the 1980s section by section, examining Fenton catalogs and other sales materials.

Changing Times, 1980-1981

A study of American handmade glass by the Society for Glass Science and Practices isolated several difficulties within the industry, ranging from increasing production costs to marketing problems. This period in Fenton's history is a time of sharp transition, as record sales and good profits eroded under rising production expenses and increasing pressures from imported giftwares.

Fenton's 1979-1980 catalog was dominated by traditional tableware and giftware glass. Hobnail was described as "an institution," and both Blue Satin and Custard Satin were traced to the nineteenth century. Opaque colors were popular, and handpainted decorations, especially roses and daisies, were well-represented, as were Violets in the Snow (DV) and Cardinals in Winter (CW) on Silver Crest glass. Fenton's Pink Blossoms on Custard Satin (PY) and Log Cabin on Custard (LC) remained in the line for some time.

The Catalog Supplement issued in January, 1980, showed New Born (NB), the Mother's day decoration, on the cover along with a new handpainted scenic decoration, Sunset (SS). Don Fenton's letter noted that 1980 marked Fenton's 75th anniversary and explained that glass produced in the 1980s would bear the Fenton oval logo with a small "8" added below the word "Fenton".

Naturally, some glass shipped in 1980 was produced in 1979 and had just the Fenton oval logo. From January 1, 1980, onward, however, all ware produced was supposed to carry the new mark. There were occasional lapses when a mould was overlooked, and the absence of the correct logo was detected only after some glassware had been produced.

The January 1980 Catalog Supplement marked the introduction of several new colors and new decorations. Crystal glass (CY) items were offered in both Daisy and Button and Fine Cut and Block; these sold well, particularly in the East and Northeast areas. Several Hobnail pieces were shown in amethyst Carnival (CN), and others seemed imminent, for the catalog noted that "the depth of selection in Fenton Hobnail is tremendous." These Carnival items were good sellers, and more pieces soon came into the line.

Two opaque colors made a half century earlier—Jade Green (JA) and Peking Blue (PK)—were revived by Fenton, but they did not sell well this time, perhaps because gift shop patrons were not enthusiastic about the contemporary colors. There were production problems, and Jade Green and Peking Blue were dropped from the line about six months later.

French Opalescent (FO) was in the line (bells only), and the Lily of the Valley pattern was also offered in Topaz Opalescent (TO). Several assortments of bells inspired by old patterns were offered in four opalescent colors. Two new handpainted decorations, Sunset (SS) and Blue Dogwood (BD), were introduced on Cameo Satin glass. The Blue Dogwood samples pictured had five petals, but the design was soon changed to the botanically correct four petals (mindful of this, some collectors now eagerly seek the short-lived five petal version).

Fenton's June 1980 catalog supplement introduced Velva Rose (VR). This was a revival of so-called "stretch glass," a treatment begun about 1917. Fenton had not made it since the 1920s-30s. Velva Rose was marketed during the last half of 1980 to commemorate Fenton's 75th anniversary. Pieces are marked with the Fenton oval logo containing the small "8", and "75th" appears just outside the oval. Many items have the onionskin-like effect created when they are brought to final shape after being sprayed with a solution of metallic salts for the iridescent finish.

The success of Velva Rose led to Velva Blue (VB), which was introduced in mid-1981. Although there were several new colors and many new decorations, the 1981-82 catalog led with ten pages of Milk Glass (mostly Hobnail), followed by Ruby ("the top selling non-opaque color"). Opalescent glass was again prominent in the Lily of the Valley pattern, and an attractive decorated opalescent glass was offered, Strawberries on French Opalescent (SF), designed by Linda Everson. The decoration caught on immediately, and additional items joined the line.

Many of the various Rose decorations (Roses on Custard, Roses on Ruby, Blue Roses etc.) remained in the line, as did Pink Blossom. The dogwood motif was available on blown Burmese items as Pink Dogwood

Fenton logo on glass made in the 1980s.

(continued on page 20)

9056 VR
BUD VASE

7527 VR
FOOTED COMPORT

7572 VR
CANDLEHOLDER

9422 VR
PERSIAN MEDALLION
COMPORT

7551 VR
DOLPHIN FAN VASE

7536 VR
8½" BASKET

7529 VR
NUT DISH

7526 VR
6½" BOWL

8408 VR
PERSIAN MEDALLION 3 PC.
FAIRY LIGHT

7516 VR
SALVER

Velva Rose (VR) was made for Fenton's 75th anniversary in 1980.

Fenton Burmese

Pure gold, uranium and another precious metal are used to achieve this exotic glass color. Each hand painted piece is proudly signed by the artist.

7506 PD
HANGING SWAG LAMP

7559 PD
7½" VASE

7552 PD
SMALL TULIP VASE

7560 PD
6½" VASE

9301 PD
20" COLUMN LAMP

7501 PD
3 PC. FAIRY LIGHT

7255 PD
LARGE TULIP VASE

In Fenton's 1981-82 catalog, Burmese glass was shown with handpainted pink dogwood flowers.

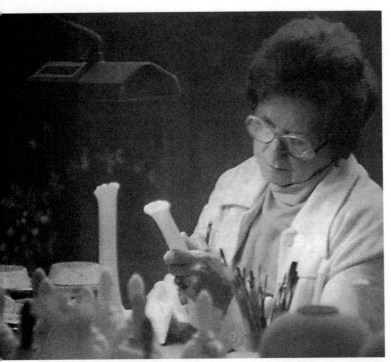

Louise Piper created many Fenton decorations before retiring in 1989 at age 81 (she passed away in 1995).

on Burmese (PD). Lamps decorated with chickadees (CQ) were offered, and two lamps in Butterflies and Bamboo (YB) were also made. The most dramatic new decoration was designer Michael Dickinson's Mountain Reflections (MV).

Although Peking Blue and Jade Green had been dropped, many shapes made in these hues were available in new colors or treatments. The Temple Jars came in Ebony (BK) as well as the interesting Silver Poppies on Ebony (PE), which was designed by Louise Piper. Many of the Silver Poppies pieces in the line were handpainted by decorator Diane Gessel. Solid figurines were available in Blue Satin, and the 8251 Mandarin Vase and 8252 Empress Vase were available in two decorated versions: Ivory on Cameo Satin (HI) or Blue on Cameo Satin (HU).

The June, 1981, catalog supplement contained limited edition Christmas articles (see Chapter Twenty-One) as well as other seasonal items. Foremost were three decorated Nativity Scene items—9401 fairy light, 9412 plate and 9463 bell—available in Antique Blue (TB), Antique Green (TG), Florentine Blue (FT), and Florentine Brown (FL) as well as Crystal Velvet. Bells and fairy lights in Ruby and Custard Satin were available with handpainted holly decorations (RH and CH, respectively). Fenton also presented hurricane shades and accompanying bases in Ruby (RU), Chestnut (NT), Butterscotch (BT) and Crystal (CY). These were purchased from a firm in Indiana which used its secret process to impart the color. Mike Fenton recalls that they moved quite well for a time and then "sales just stopped!"

In the fall of 1981, Fenton's special assortment was "Country pitchers from Fenton country." There were pitchers and cruets in four colors—Amethyst (AY), Blue (BB), Country Cranberry (CC) and Ruby (RU)—and many were among the new articles offered in the January 1982 Catalog Supplement. CC was a new color code, and the glass was somewhat darker and more intense than

Fenton's Ruby Overlay (RO), which was made from 1943 to 1974. Fenton's chemists developed Country Cranberry in the summer of 1981, and the color was put in the line shortly thereafter.

In the fall of 1981, Fenton placed advertising in these national publications: *Americana; Christmas Ideas; Country Living; Early American Life; House Beautiful; McCall's;* and *Southern Living*. The company's glassware sales were good at the moment, but the next several years were to bring difficult times.

The Pressure Builds, 1982-1984

During 1982-1984, Fenton experienced downturns in both sales and profits, even though it sought some new directions with contemporary design. The Fenton Catalog Supplement for January, 1982, is a mixture of traditional and contemporary, and both Katja and American Legacy (see Chapter Nineteen) debuted later that year. Those familiar with Fenton history may recall the contemporary designs introduced in the 1950s. "New World" (designed by Stan Fistick) came out in 1953, and Michael Lax's "Horizon" appeared about six years later.

Fenton's traditional glassware continued the "country" emphasis, which was a popular marketplace theme in 1982. Two pages each were devoted to Country Cranberry (CC) and Country Peach (RT). These and other colors—Amethyst (AY) and Forget-Me-Not Blue (KL)—were couched in similar terms ("for warmth and beauty"). Crystal (in patterns such as Strawberries, Panelled Daisy or Button and Arch) was dubbed the "Country Crystal Collection," and the hen covered dishes were called "Country Hens." These retailed well in the early 1980s, and other glass manufacturers, such as Imperial, were also marketing crystal successfully.

The Fenton theme of "traditional" ware was also articulated in three picture frames (ware numbers 7594, 7595 and 7596) as well as the 9504 candlelight and 9574 chamberstick, all of which were available in several colors and with a variety of handpainted decorations. The frames had begun as special orders for Burnes of Boston, and they were made for them in other colors and treatments before being put into the Fenton line.

Two new decorations were introduced—Vintage (VI) on Cameo Satin and Blue Garland (GA) on Custard Satin—but they did not sell well. In fact, almost all of Fenton's once-popular handpainted floral motifs on opaque satin glass were not selling well. In retrospect, Don Fenton termed these "tired," and other family members readily agree.

On the contemporary side, Fenton's innovative Sculptured Ice Optics consisted of nine vases and a 12" bowl, all of which were available in crystal as well as Amethyst (AY) and Glacial Blue (BB). Most of the shapes were also made in Country Cranberry. The Sculptured Ice Optics were difficult to make and remained in the line for less than a year.

The Iris Collection was Fenton's other innovative direction. A pink iris was handpainted on bone white glass (IN), and Richard Delaney's iris design was also sandcarved on six different Amethyst items (IY). These were the first sandcarved items in the line (for more on sandcarving, see Chapter Twenty-Three).

Elaborate sandcarving on Fenton's Ebony glass was featured with three Sophisticated Ladies (SX) vases pro-

Designed by Linda Everson, the Dianthus on Custard (DN) handpainted decoration was shown in Fenton's 1983-84 catalog.

duced under an agreement (initiated by Fenton's Pat Clark) with the Duke Ellington Project Partnership. The design was based on a *Playbill* program for the popular musical, which was running in New York and Los Angeles. These were licensed items, and Fenton paid royalties to the Ellington group.

Another new color, Cobalt Blue (KB), was available in 1982. Some articles were sandcarved (KY), while others were handpainted with a Morning Glories motif (KP). Among the new handpainted decorations were Mike Dickinson's Down by the Station (TT) on Cameo Satin and Diane Johnson's Wildflowers (FD). The catalog described Wildflowers as "understated elegance...silvery white and rich brown." The colors were perhaps a bit too understated, however, and customer suggestions were taken to heart in a "New Improved Wildflowers" released in late July, 1983.

Fenton's Catalog Supplement for May, 1982, introduced Christmas articles and extended the line in other areas. Nativity Scene plates and bells were available decorated in Antique Dark Brown (TD) as well as a "brighter" Florentine (FL). The crystal and colored hurricane lamps were embellished with sandcarved decorations in the form of Love Birds (LQ) or Poinsettias (PN), and Astral Candlelights were also offered.

The Katja/Fenton and American Legacy lines debuted in the late fall of 1982 (see Chapter Nineteen). Fenton used the American Legacy colors (Amethyst, Candleglow Yellow, Federal Blue and Heritage Green) for special promotions, such as the 9134 Butterfly and Berry basket and the 9280 Butterfly/Rose candy box. In the fall-winter, the popular Federal Blue color was used

for eight Regency pattern pieces; these were also offered in crystal.

The Regency ware was made in moulds which had been purchased from the Jeannette Glass Company, but many of them can be traced back to the McKee firm early in the twentieth century. Regency was originally McKee's "Plytec" line. Fenton's purchase involved about 2,000 moulds, and some of them—such as Vulcan articles (e.g., 9551 covered candy box) and the 8625 Puritan comport—were important later in the 1980s.

Despite the enthusiasm for the new articles and colors in the fall of 1982, however, all was not well. A month before the New York show where Katja/Fenton and An American Legacy were to be introduced, Don Fenton advised Fenton reps that 273 articles ("the largest number of items ever") would be discontinued from the Fenton line. This included all items in Burmese, Cameo Opalescent, Carnival, Velva Blue and Velva Rose as well as many articles in crystal, Forget-Me-Not Blue and Country Peach. The Sculptured Ice Optic group was dropped, along with all items in such decorations as Blue Garland, Blue Roses, Chocolate Roses, and Mountain Reflections. The Silver Poppies on Ebony items were eliminated from the line along with the sandcarved Sophisticated Ladies.

In the mid-1980s, Fenton began to introduce groups of 12-15 items in Carnival glass. Each group was offered for a year before being retired. The 1983 offering consisted of nine items in amethyst Carnival (CN) glass as well as the 8417 CN Currier and Ives "Harvest" plate, which was limited to 3500.

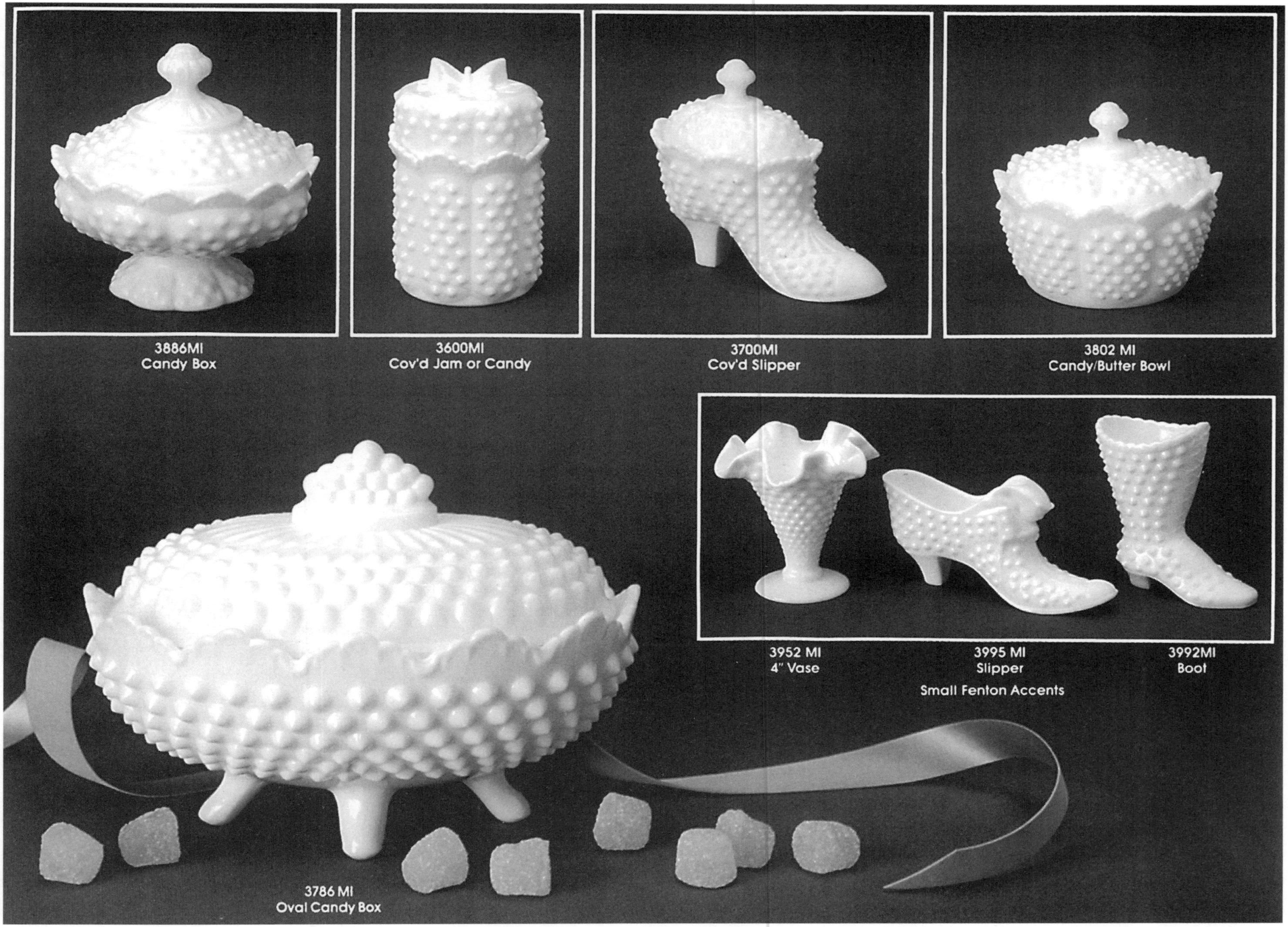

Milk Glass Hobnail items from Fenton's 1983-84 catalog.

3886MI
Candy Box

3600MI
Cov'd Jam or Candy

3700MI
Cov'd Slipper

3802 MI
Candy/Butter Bowl

3786 MI
Oval Candy Box

3952 MI
4" Vase

3995 MI
Slipper

Small Fenton Accents

3992MI
Boot

In 1983, this mark was added to moulds Fenton purchased from other glass companies, such as McKee (this mark is not used in the moulds purchased earlier from Paden City, Verlys or the U. S. Glass Co.).

Fenton's 1983-84 catalog was smaller than the last two versions, and the first four pages were devoted to Crystal Velvet. A page headed "Famous Fenton Color" contains this paragraph: "Always well-known for color—be it rich and resplendent or gently soft pastels—Fenton is especially proud of its latest offering in transparent glass. Taking our direction from the color experts in the home fashion industry, each of our new colors has been developed to appeal to the taste of today's consumer. Four months of market testing helped us to refine our original choices to bring you the most exciting group of transparent colors in the handmade glass industry."

Although four of the six colors—Amethyst, Candleglow Yellow, Country Peach, Federal Blue, Forget-Me-Not Blue and Heritage Green—had been introduced with American Legacy, the new catalog showed a wide variety of items. Three colors were available as "overlays" with an opal core—Federal Blue Overlay (OF), Heritage Green Overlay (OH) and Yellow Overlay (OY). There were just five different shapes for these overlay colors, but the use of optic moulds (fern, feather or spiral) added variety.

Amethyst was still available with the sandcarved iris motif, and Cobalt Blue was produced with two sandcarved motifs, Lovebirds (LK) and Butterfly (KY) as well as two handpainted decorations, Morning Glories (KP) and Straw Flowers (SQ). The sandcarved Cobalt Blue pieces had white paint added for extra definition. Both Ruby and Country Cranberry were well-represented, and the latter became a strong seller. Ten new pieces were offered in Carnival glass. Six pages of crystal highlighted the Regency and Strawberry patterns as well as Glass Pets. In decorated ware, Fenton was enthusiastic about the brighter colors of Linda Everson's Dianthus on Custard (DN) and Frosted Asters on Blue Satin (FA).

Assortments of bells ranged from 8-piece "Spring" assortments composed of hand-decorated 6½" bells or petite bells to a 39-piece assortment of bells in various sizes, colors and decorations. A letter to Fenton reps (dated December 7, 1982) noted that the "petite" bells had been particularly strong sellers during the past year.

The Fenton Catalog Supplement for June, 1983, served mainly to introduce the Connoisseur Collection (see Chapter Twenty), the Designer Series and the Christmas Fantasy Series (see Chapter Twenty-One). There were, however, other items, such as the decal-decorated Budweiser Clydesdales (XA). The catalog supplement

also pictured decorated Fawns (codes RD, XP and XW) and Petite Bells and Ornaments (codes XR, XX and XG).

In November, a flyer introduced the forthcoming "Romantic Country." Created by Linda Everson and called Berries and Blossoms (RK), this decoration featured tiny handpainted raspberries and blooms as well as pale pink "blush" on the rims or edges of the Opal Satin pieces. Berries and Blossoms became a strong seller, and this motif marks the turning point in Fenton's attempts to recapture the earlier popularity of decorated ware.

Fenton's January 1984 Supplement began with three pages devoted to popular items such as Glass Pets and animal figurines. A group called Prayer Children included the Praying Boy and Girl figurines as well as bells, electrified lights and mugs. The overlay colors were extended by five new shapes (four vases and an apple made off-hand), and a new hue, Dusty Rose Overlay (OD). The Romantic Country group had two catalog pages showing Berries and Blossoms and a single page devoted to handpainted Petite Fleur (PF), which consisted of "tiny blue periwinkles scattered over an opaline glass." Both Petite Fleur and Berries and Blossoms were described as "Country French."

Cobalt Marigold Carnival (NK) and transparent Dusty Rose (DK) debuted in the January, 1984, Supplement. The Carnival color was made with a marigold spray on Fenton's Cobalt Blue glass. The new Dusty Rose transparent color was described as "beautiful and unusual in its depth and richness," and Fenton dealers were urged to display Dusty Rose with articles in Dusty Rose Overlay or with one of the decorated Romantic Country motifs, Petite Fleur or Berries and Blossoms. The catalog supplement pictured 14 different articles in Dusty Rose.

Dusty Rose became one of Fenton's most popular colors in the 1980s. By March, 1984, Fenton had put together special product assortments in which Dusty Rose was combined with Dusty Rose Overlay and the handpainted Berries and Blossoms Fenton dealers got 16 pieces of glass plus color-coordinated fabric, ribbon and flowers to use in displays (this successful idea was used several times during 1984).

Dusty Rose was still in the line at the end of 1990,

These "hand swung accents" (9635 6" basket, 9659 7½" swung vase and 9671 4½" swung votive) were available in Dusty Rose (DK), Federal Blue (FB) and Heritage Green (HG) in 1984.

and it was featured in brochures depicting assortments with Fenton's Christine Victoria. In terms of unit sales volume, Dusty Rose was Fenton's number one color of the 1980s (a more expensive color, Country Cranberry, was number one in sales dollars).

The origin of Dusty Rose is difficult to pinpoint. Fenton chemist Subodh Gupta had made experimental melts of various pinks, and Wayne King continued these trials. He had developed Dusty Rose in pot glass when it entered the line. As the color became increasingly popular, Wayne worked out batches that could be made in Fenton's larger day tanks.

The Catalog Supplement for May 1984 introduced pieces in the Designer Series and the Connoisseur Series as well as Christmas gift items. Among the latter were the 9673 Santa Votive and the 7275 footed votive in various colors as well as attractive animal figurines. The animals were described as "merry little mice, well mannered mallards and the oh-so-cool cats." A new Christmas decoration, Winter (XT), was available on various bells and candleholders.

Market Segments, 1985-86

Well before the 1985 sales season, the company made important changes in its marketing. In 1983-84, Fenton's management worked closely with the Richardson/Smith consulting firm of Worthington, Ohio. In addition to developing a new logo (the large script "F") and slogan ("A Continuing Celebration in Fine Glass") for Fenton, the consultants conducted a series of "audits" of Fenton's products, promotional materials and distribution network. These audits helped Fenton focus upon developing short-term and long-term goals in design, marketing and sales. As a result of Richardson/Smith's work with Fenton, the line was "segmented" into three distinct divisions—Artisan, Classic and Spotlight—and separate catalogs would be issued, although all glassware would be sold through the same reps.

On another front, Fenton was faced with a decision regarding its presence in New York City, then the epicenter of the giftware trade. Since 1961, Fenton's ware had been shown in the New York City showroom of Howard B. Aronow, who represented several glassware manufacturers. His lease was almost at its end, and Aronow was

The Glass Pets were featured in Fenton's 1985-86 Classic catalog.

24

The Country Bouquet (FX) decoration was shown in Fenton's 1985-86 Spotlight catalog.

going to retire. Fenton management decided to assume Aronow's lease and to remodel the showroom in the Gift Center (225 Fifth Avenue, Room 506) as an exclusive display for its products. In 1984, the facility was redesigned by Richardson/Smith's John McCulley to use flexible modules and neutral backgrounds which would emphasize the colors of the glass on display.

Fenton reps met at the newly-opened showroom on November 9, 1984, to hear plans for the 1985 sales season and to attend the annual New York Tabletop and Accessory Show. Shortly thereafter, in a letter to Fenton retailers, Bill Fenton was candid about the industry and Fenton's plans for the future: "For almost 80 years, Fenton has supplied fine glassware to America's retailers. With the departure of certain American handglass names, you may have wondered how Fenton can succeed when so many others have failed."

Bill outlined Fenton's plans for 1985, which entailed "glass for three separate marketing segments." These were Classic (glassware for "traditional gift and card

shops, jewelry stores and department stores"), Artisan ("contemporary department stores and specialty shops") and Spotlight ("lower priced 'fun' items").

The Classic division, regarded as "the backbone of the Fenton success story for many years, both past and future," was featured in a 48-page catalog. Eight pages were devoted to Milk Glass, including both Hobnail and Silver Crest, and other Fenton colors were well-represented—Periwinkle Blue and Periwinkle Blue Overlay; Dusty Rose and Dusty Rose Overlay; Country Cranberry; Ruby; and Cobalt Marigold Carnival. Among the new colors were Gray Mist (GF) and Sunset Peach (FE).

Periwinkle Blue and Periwinkle Blue Overlay were coordinated with the handpainted Autumn Leaves and Meadow Blooms (LB), and Dusty Rose and Dusty Rose Overlay were linked with Blossoms and Berries. Other handpainted decorations included Frosted Asters, Blossom and Berries and Pink Blossom. The series of Natural Animals, first introduced in 1984, was expanded to an even dozen.

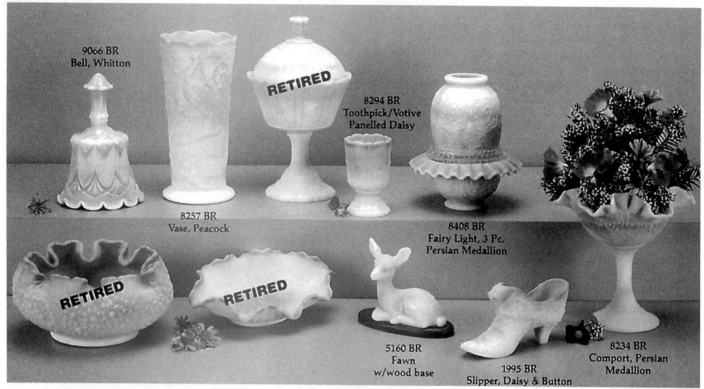

These articles in Fenton's pressed Burmese were made in 1986. Those designated "retired" (9185 BR Panelled Daisy covered candy, 8289 Orange Tree and Cherry crimped bowl and 9125 BR oval dish) were sold out when this illustration appeared in the 1987-88 catalog.

Fenton's Artisan pieces were intended for department stores "which cater to a non-traditional market." These stores wanted "dramatic, contemporary styling," and they had turned to European products. The Artisan pieces proved reasonably successful in terms of sales, but Fenton's customers wanted new offerings twice per year and the company found this difficult to sustain.

There were two Artisan groupings, Geometrics and the Masterworks Collection. The Geometrics were designed by Richard Delaney. An Art Deco-style motif was etched on several different transparent colors (Dusty Rose, Gray Mist or Periwinkle Blue) to create vases with a strong contemporary look.

The Masterworks consisted of three blown shapes in cased glass. Beginning with a core of colored glass, the gatherer covered it with a milk glass or gray overlay. A skilled finisher applied thin threads and a colored "dot" before the article was covered with a layer of crystal and blown to final shape. There were four Masterworks color codes: KM (cobalt blue interior, milk glass exterior with two stripes and a blue dot); NV (navy blue interior, gray exterior with two stripes and a blue dot); TV (teal interior, gray exterior with two stripes and a teal dot); and UV (ruby interior, gray exterior with two stripes and a ruby dot). One of Fenton's most highly-skilled glassworkers, Delmer Stowasser, was responsible for the design of the Masterworks Collection.

Fenton's low-priced Spotlight items were intended for both regular accounts and all sorts of other stores. Fenton hoped that these "additional sales channels" would boost volume. The Spotlight catalog featured low-priced "impulse items" such as ring trees, votives and nut dishes as well as crystal Glass Pets. Other Spotlight items, such as the Barnyard Buddies bells and a five-piece

Country Bouquet group, were decorated by pad printing, as were the Campbell Kids bells and the three-piece Teddy Bear collection.

Another Spotlight item, the Luv Bug, played a role in Fenton's 1985 Valentine's Day promotion. For several years in the early 1980s, Fenton had highlighted ruby or various pink colors for Valentine's Day. For 1985, however, Fenton conceived and developed an entirely new product, the Luv Bug. The shops achieved remarkable production, and "The Fenton World" newsletter (February 1985) credited pressers Dave Vincent and Ron Dick with an average of 1311 pieces per turn. One exceptional turn yielded about 1600 pieces, far above the threshold for incentive pay.

The crystal Luv Bug, which retailed for $7.50, came in an ingenious, attractive package designed by Lebanon Packaging. A countertop display unit holding a dozen individually-packaged Luv Bugs was developed. When the "door" on the package was opened, the Luv Bug peered out through the opening. Stickers gave the buyer a choice of messages, ranging from Valentine's Day ("I'm buggy over you") or birthday ("Happy birthday to someone who always stands out from the swarm") to generic thinking-of-you ("Haven't heard from you in a cocoon's age. Bug me sometime.").

Although the Luv Bug was promoted to stationery stores and other non-traditional outlets for Fenton products, the item proved unattractive and its sales performance was disappointing. Other Spotlight items such as the Glass Pets, however, sold well. From the company's standpoint, however, it was difficult to develop low-priced items which could be made economically in a hand operation.

In April 1985, Fenton's re-introduced Blue Ridge (BI) in honor of the firm's 80th anniversary. This ware has a cobalt blue "crest" on French opalescent glass, a combination first effected about 1938 by Fenton glassworker Pete Raymond. These ten Blue Ridge items were marked with the Fenton oval logo as well as "80th". Blue Ridge was in the line only during 1985, although perfume bottles later appeared in the 1986 Connoisseur Collection.

In anticipation of Christmas, Fenton prepared a special mailing in March 1985. The Classic line was extended with the 5107 Madonna Prayer Light and the 5112 Praying Angels two-piece set. These were produced in Crystal Velvet as well as handpainted versions. A 20-piece "Winter" assortment was also available, as were groups of decorated musical bells. Some of the popular Glass Pets were dressed up with red/green bows to make them "Holiday Pets." A pad printed motif called Kissing Santas (SN) was applied to bells, candleholders and oval baskets; these were marketed as the Christmas Happiness assortment.

In 1986, Fenton issued a single catalog, but it mirrored the three divisions (Artisan, Classic and Spotlight). Fenton reps preferred one complete catalog to three separate booklets. Several of the new opalescent colors—French Cream (FO), Minted Cream (EO) and Peaches 'N Cream (UO)—appeared in both the Artisan and the Classic sections. These were described as "delectable ice cream colors," and, in the Artisan section, large vases, baskets, bowls and other articles were shown under the aegis "Reflections."

Some of the shapes from the Geometrics group were used for Richard Delaney's new concept, Silhouettes (EK). These black vases were individually masked and sprayed with 24k gold using an airbrush "to create the dreamlike imagery of Japanese Contemporary." Richard describes the effect as "rather haunting ...as if you're looking into it and looking back at yourself at the same time."

The Classic section featured Fenton's traditional hues—Milk Glass (including Silver Crest), Carnival, and Ruby—as well as the increasingly popular Dusty Rose and Periwinkle Blue along with their overlay counterparts. In handpainted decorations, Thistles and Bows (EW) joined Meadow Blooms and Pink Blossom.

The Classic section also showcased more than a dozen items in pressed Burmese (BR) with a sandblasted satin finish. The Burmese color had appeared in the initial Connoisseur Collection in 1983 (7562 UF handpainted bell and 7605 BR epergne).

The small Spotlight section was dominated by low-priced gift suggestions (Glass Pets, bells and votives) and

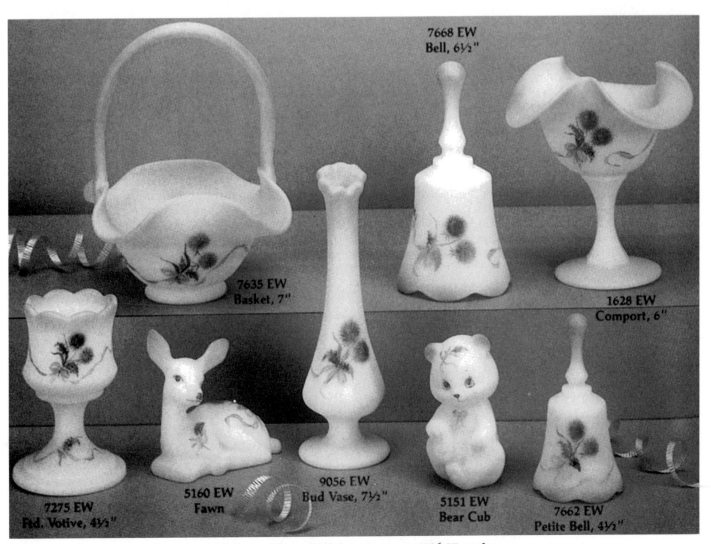

7668 EW
Bell, 6½"

7635 EW
Basket, 7"

1628 EW
Comport, 6"

7275 EW
Ftd. Votive, 4½"

5160 EW
Fawn

9056 EW
Bud Vase, 7½"

5151 EW
Bear Cub

7662 EW
Petite Bell, 4½"

Thistles and Bows (EW) from Fenton's 1986-87 catalog.

9658 NK
Vase, Dogwood, 8" h.

9234 NK
Basket, Butterfly & Berry

*Cobalt Marigold
Carnival*

9276 NK
Comport, Ftd.,
Innovation

9279 NK
Comport, 7",
Marquette

9653 NK
Rose Bowl, Fabergé

5148 NK
Mouse

5119 NK
Kitten

8289 NK
Bowl, Orange Tree & Cherry

8361 NK
Bell, Barred Oval

Cobalt Marigold Carnival glass items from Fenton's 1986-87 catalog.

a series of pieces intended for 25th or 50th anniversaries (the glassware was purchased from other companies, and Fenton decorated it with decals and applied gold bands). The Country Bouquet assortment and the pad printed Teddy Bear musical bell were also in the Spotlight section.

Opalescent glass was emphasized by Fenton throughout 1986. The Valentine's day promotion consisted of seven pieces in French Opalescent and two pieces in this same hue enhanced by a rose decoration (KR). In June, an assortment of Victorian -style, blown creamers and cruets was promoted. These were made with several different optic patterns to enhance the effect, and Cobalt Opalescent (KF, cobalt blue cased with French Opalescent) was added.

By mid-1986, animal figurines emerged as a popular staple among Fenton collectibles. These ranged from Glass Pets in crystal or Crystal Velvet to the colorful, all-over decorated Natural Animals. The "True Blue Friends" (IK) animals were introduced in the June, 1986, catalog supplement, which described them as "two different glasses...joined together by hand [and]...iridized with a secret formula while the glass is still hot." Small quantities of Fenton's cobalt blue glass were gathered from a pot and placed within a ring in another pot containing milk glass. A glassworker then gathered the proper cobalt blue/milk glass combination and dropped it into the press mould. After pressing, the pieces were iridized.

When the Fenton reps gathered in Williamstown in late 1986, they learned that the company would place renewed emphasis upon handled baskets and Milk Glass Hobnail. More than 200 new items were added to the line, and price reductions of 10 to 23% made some items and assortments particularly attractive to Fenton dealers.

Basics and Bears, 1987-1990

In a letter to Fenton customers dated January 5, 1987, Don Fenton articulated the company's theme for 1987: "Back to Basics." This slogan, reflecting an emphasis on traditional shapes and successful colors, shaped the line for the remainder of the decade. This refocusing (and strong sales of the Birthstone Bears) changed Fenton's fortunes.

More than 200 new items appeared in Fenton's 1987-88 catalog, and, to stimulate orders, Fenton lowered prices on many popular items. Basket prices were reduced 15%, and the minimum order was increased from one to two.

The 1987-88 Fenton catalog had a strong emphasis on two colors—the well-established Dusty Rose and a relative newcomer, Provincial Blue Opalescent (OO). Dealers were urged to combine Dusty Rose with a decorated opal satin called Victorian Roses (VJ) as well as Dusty Rose Overlay. Victorian Roses also harmonized with Fenton's Country Cranberry color. Provincial Blue Opalescent could be combined with another decorated opal satin, Provincial Bouquet (FS).

Milk Glass Hobnail occupied three full pages, and a revived color, Colonial Amber (CA) was accorded a full page. There were several bell assortments, ranging from the handpainted Botanical Bells to a comprehensive 34-bell group that encompassed most of the colors and treatments from the line. The catalog devoted a full page to Natural Animals, and other low-priced offerings included assortments of the 5197 Happiness Bird along

Fenton's Birthstone Bears display unit.

with various votives, vases and novelty items. The anniversary pieces were strengthened by a decoration which read simply "Happy Anniversary" without reference to a particular year.

A report in late March, 1987, listed Dusty Rose and Provincial Blue Opalescent as Fenton's top two colors during the first several months of the year, with Country Cranberry, Milk Glass and Ruby occupying ranks four through six. The Victorian Roses decoration stood third, and Provincial Bouquet was seventh. The Anniversary pieces were also moving well, standing second among the "Top Looks," just behind Dusty Rose/Victorian Roses. In unit sales, Dusty Rose and Provincial Blue Opalescent articles, particularly baskets, occupied 16 slots in the "Top 20" list, including the top seven positions. Several figurines (5127 Swan and 5197 Happiness Bird) were among the top ten items, too. These trends continued, and Dusty Rose, Provincial Blue Opalescent and Country Cranberry were Fenton's 1-2-3 top-selling colors for the first six months of 1987.

The June, 1987, catalog supplement introduced some low-priced items pad printed with a Biblical verse in gold script and handpainted floral decorations—Floral Spray (FR) or Lovely Lilies (LR). These were the beginning of Fenton's entry into the "inspirational" market, and other articles were developed. In December, 1987, Fenton notified its reps that OMCO of Grand Rapids, Michigan, would "represent Fenton to the religious bookstore market." Don's memo noted that Fenton had been "studying [this market] for over a year now" and concluded that "it is a very specialized market and one we feel can no longer be overlooked."

June, 1987, also marked the catalog debut of the Birthstone Bears. This product was developed over a long period, as Fenton pondered astrological and zodiac ideas before settling on a birthday gift article. The figurines (Fenton's 5151 bear cub) are "adorned with a birthstone heart" representing individual months. Messages designed to "personalize" the Birthstone Bear for each month were written, such as the following: "Salutations from February Bear. I'm the intellectual type. Smarter than the average Birthday Bear! I'm also thrifty, but I'm worth every penny!" The catalog supplement showed a large photo of the October Bear with Rose Zircon heart, and dealers were offered two dozen bears (2 for each month) and a two-tier display unit. These had wide appeal, even among dealers who didn't sell colored glass.

The colored hearts are attached using a glue which sets when exposed to ultraviolet light. Early samples were made using ruby hearts from an imported novelty "tree" stocked by the Fenton Gift Shop. These had faceted surfaces and were difficult to attach properly. Another problem to be overcome was that of obtaining hearts in all twelve birthstone hues. For a time, the company purchased crystal hearts and lustered them to create the proper colors. Ultimately, Fenton purchased quantities of flat hearts in the proper birthstone colors from the Swarovski Jewelry Company.

The first six months of 1987, sales were up over 20% compared to 1986, and a backlog of orders led Fenton's management to schedule additional production. Fenton-From-Afar and Christine Victoria had been well-received at recent shows. Although the glassmaking operation was not yet yielding profits, sales in the Fenton Gift Shop (a separate corporation from the Fenton Art Glass Glass Company) were encouraging. Total glass sales for 1987 were up 15%, and Christine Victoria was selling very well.

In retrospect, George Fenton attributes the company's turnaround to designing better products and to more aggressive sales strategies, especially the market

Two Floral Dreams (FF) vases were shown with a Country Cranberry basket in Fenton's 1989 catalog.

29

presentation of Christine Victoria with Fenton glass. George also noted the growth of Fenton's special products department (see Chapter Twenty-Three) and that a weaker U. S. dollar helped turn the tide on imports.

Fenton's commitment to the "Back to Basics" theme was evident in catalogs from 1988 and 1989. Several new Fenton colors and decorations extended the emphasis on pinks and blues, and some had an iridescent treatment. Shell Pink (PE) was described as a "soft opal glass with a pearl finish," and the Hearts and Flowers (FH) decoration featured handpainted pink roses on iridized opal glass.

A deep cobalt blue called Blue Royale (KK) made its debut in 1988, as did the aquamarine Teal Royale (OC). Both were available as overlays (with opal glass) in Fenton lamps. Teal Royale also served as the base color for the iridescent Teal Marigold (OI).

In mid-May, 1988, Don Fenton reported to Fenton's reps that sales through them from January-April were up 34%. A mailing to about 15,000 Fenton accounts was scheduled for early June. The Christine Victoria operation was preparing to move from California to nearby Vienna, West Virginia, although sales of these products were experiencing a slight decline.

Fenton's January, 1989 catalog supplement showed several additions to the line, including Rose Corsage (MP), which was described as "Pearlized Shell Pink glass embellished with a beautiful porcelain rose and then handpainted." This glass was lightly iridized in Fenton's Hot Metal department prior to annealing. After the hand-painted decoration was completed and fired-on in the decorating lehr, the individual porcelain roses were applied using an epoxy glue.

The new Mulberry (MG) was described as a "blend of gold ruby and azure blue...combined to bring you an exciting lavender glass which shades to a lustrous cranberry edge." Fenton had made a Mulberry color in 1942, but this earlier color was intended to be more homogeneous, although it didn't turn out that way!

Fenton's Elizabeth Collection consisted of Silver Crest with a handpainted blue floral (ES) and Blue Royale with a handpainted white floral (EM). These items looked well together, and the January, 1989, catalog supplement urged dealers to display them with Christine Victoria items for maximum visual appeal.

Several new products impacted Fenton's bottom line quickly. At the end of the first four months of 1989, the decorated Elizabeth Collection (EM and ES) was second only to Country Cranberry. Mulberry ranked fourth, just ahead of the perennial Dusty Rose, and third place was held by Persian Blue Opalescent (XC), a color from the Fenton "Collector's Extravaganza" offerings (see Chapter Twenty-Six). In fact, the number one selling item was the 1404 Persian Blue 7-piece water set. The remainder of the best selling item list was dominated by Birthstone Bears, which occupied places two through seven. Three articles from the Elizabeth Collection were among the top 11 best sellers.

The June, 1989, catalog supplement showcased two more new products which harmonized with items from Christine Victoria. These were Copper Rose (KP), a black glass "embellished with a garland of handpainted floral splendor and accented with copper," and Antique Rose (AF), which featured handpainted roses with enamel beadwork and burnished rose edges.

During the 1980s, Fenton maintained a solid relationship with the J. C. Penney Company. Sales dimin-

Happy Santas

5239 NS
Bear, Daydreaming
4"

5220 NS
Pig, 2¾"

5233 NS
Bear, Reclining, 4"

Five Fenton animal figurines were decorated with Santa attire for assortment of "Happy Santas" in 1990.

5148 NS
Mouse, 2¾"

5151 NS
Bear, Sitting, 3½"

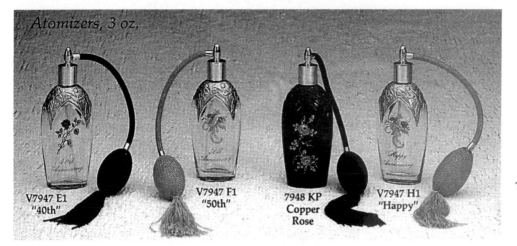

Atomizers, 3 oz.

V7947 E1 "40th"

V7947 F1 "50th"

7948 KP Copper Rose

V7947 H1 "Happy"

These atomizers appeared in Fenton's June, 1990. catalog supplement.

ished in the middle of the decade, however, and Fenton sought to rejuvenate this business. Selling Fenton glassware to major department stores is not, however, as easy as one might think, Fenton's reps had to deal with buyers for several different departments, and ordering procedures were sometimes cumbersome. Penney's corporate headquarters relocated from Manhattan to a Dallas suburb, and its buyer, Greg Engel, was developing a "country" theme. Fenton's Christine Victoria soft goods and glassware assortments fit the theme nicely and were well-received in Penney's gift departments. Sales to J. C. Penney stores nationwide increased sharply in 1989, and this effort is certainly one of Fenton's success stories from the 1980s.

Overall, 1989 was a very good year, as sales were up about 14%. Fenton continued to plan for increased production and for expansion into markets such as lighting goods and perfume bottles. The Gracious Touch party plan (see Chapter Twenty-Five) was discontinued, but Fenton glass had been selling strongly, especially through Hallmark stores, J. C. Penney's and the QVC television outlet (see Chapter Twenty-Four). The 1990 sales year also began well, and the Spring, 1990, issue of the "Fenton Forecast" newsletter reported that "sales are up 25% over 1989."

Fenton's 1990-91 catalog reflected a company secure in the present and confident of its future. Large, dramatic photos, many depicting new colors, prefaced major sections. The relatively new Copper Rose and decorated Antique Rose led the first part, which also unveiled Petal Pink (PN) with these words: "the newest color from Fenton...romantic and versatile...pretty, priced right and perfect for remembering someone special."

The catalog's second section introduced a light blue color called Salem Blue (SR) as well as Watercolors (PF), a new decoration described as "subtle pastel florals handpainted on the gentle blush of pink satin glass." Another new decoration, Country Scene (LT) depicted weathered buildings and a section of stone wall.

Two full pages of Dusty Rose anchored the third part of the catalog, accompanied by Shell Pink, Hearts and Flowers, and a decoration called Pearly Sentiments (PT), which had been introduced in the January, 1989, catalog supplement. The pearlized opal glass used for the latter was the same as that used for Hearts and Flowers. The catalog described Pearly Sentiments as "a marriage of iridescent opal glass and skillfully sculpted porcelain roses."

The next section of the 1990-91 catalog showed Mulberry opposite another decoration, Tulips (TL) on iridescent opal glass, before introducing another new color, Lilac (LX). Described as "Fenton's newest color dictated by the decorative trends that use this lovely pastel shade in fabrics and wall coverings," Lilac is reminiscent of the Wisteria color made in 1977-78.

Fenton's Country Cranberry and Ruby were shown to good advantage, as were some relative newcomers to the line, Red Carnival (RN) and a large assortment of Cranberry Opalescent (CR). The catalog copy explained that Red Carnival is "made with Ruby glass and iridized with a special metallic salt formula. Occasionally there will be unusual colorations because of the way the ruby strikes and some pieces will have an amberina effect." The Cranberry Opalescent pieces exhibited a variety of optic effects (diamond, dot, drapery, or spiral).

Although just six pages, Fenton's June,1990 supplement introduced several new things. The company's 85th anniversary was marked by decorated Burmese items (RB Rose Burmese; QH Raspberry Burmese; QJ Petite Floral; and QD Tree Scene). This "Anniversary Offering" actually comprised the Connoisseur Collection for 1990 (see Chapter Twenty).

Two new cased glass colors, Cranberry Opaline (KH) and Cased Jade Opaline (AG) debuted, as did another hue, Jade Opaline (AP). The inner layer of these Cranberry Opaline bowls and vases is a lush red, contrasting beautifully with the pale opal exterior. Cased Jade Opaline is made by a similar process, and pieces also vary in color intensity. Jade Opaline is an opalescent glass, and collectors will find it similar to Fenton's blue opalescent wares, albeit with greenish tones added.

The Line in Retrospect

"Oh, Fenton. You're the people who do that white glass with the funny bumps." The department store buyer in 1984 was both right and wrong. Fenton did indeed make Milk Glass Hobnail, but the company was anxiously searching for new directions with contemporary designs. Fenton's image was strongly associated with traditional glassware, however, and the giftware marketplace was teeming with competition, both foreign and domestic. The first six years of the 1980s were very difficult times.

After several years of trying other directions, Fenton went back to basics and developed new products, such

Fenton Handlers' Marks

Ron Bayles
(1956-current)

Fred Bruce
(1953-1990)

Bob Buchanan
(1990-current)

D. Austin Dallison
(1933-1982)

Terry Deuley
(1989-current)

Brian Green
(1986-current)

Lloyd Lauderman
(1953-1993)

Robert Oliver, Sr.
(1957-1995)

Bob Patterson
(1973-current)

J. R. Phillips
(1986-1995)

Delmer Stowasser
(1965-1990)

Junior Thompson
(1955-77 and 1990-93)

Dave Vincent
(1964-current)

Butch Wright
(1973-current)

Each Fenton basket has an individual handler's mark where the handle is attached.
These marks were used by those skilled craftsmen who worked during the 1980-1990 period.
The marks are shown, and the dates of each man's employment are given.

as the Birthstone Bear and other "sentiment" items as well as impulse items (votives, bells and slippers). Home fashion colors were used, and traditional styles and shapes regained their niche among customers. The Dusty Rose and Country Cranberry colors proved popular and durable throughout the last half of the decade. These products—plus the seasonal offerings for Valentine's Day, Easter and Christmas—allowed reps to make regular visits to their accounts with a ready answer to the constant question "What's new?"

Fenton catalogs (both for glassware and Christine Victoria) emphasized the coordinating colors in their page layout and presentation. Multi-piece assortments and display concepts were created so that Fenton reps could sell to wholesale customers more easily. At the retail level, the company's name recognition was enhanced by "hang tags" which told customers the Fenton story of handmade glass and, on baskets, described the individual handler's marks.

Fenton's turnaround can be linked to several other factors. Color statements became integral to everything from glass design to suggestions for retail store displays. Fenton's design philosophy changed as trends in color marketing were closely monitored, and decorations were developed for both transparent and opaque glass which coordinated with other colors in the company's line.

Chapter Nineteen
NEW CONCEPTS:
KATJA and AMERICAN LEGACY

In 1981, the American home furnishings industry was increasingly interested in "concept" merchandise. The concept idea, pioneered by Gear Inc., is simple enough: a designer (or design team) creates a multitude of products (fabrics, paint, wallcoverings, cookwares) to be manufactured by firms (called licensees), which pay royalties to the designer. The products are sold in department stores or specialty shops which establish areas where the "concept" (i. e., all the different products in proximity) can be seen by shoppers. The color schemes emphasize coordination rather than exact matches, so harmonious looks can be achieved in the home—dining room, kitchen, bath, bedroom, etc.

Several major department stores—Macy's (New York and San Francisco), Foley's, Burdine's, Lazarus, and Carson Pirie Scott—were displaying concept wares designed by Raymond Waites, Nigel French and Laura Ashley. In August, 1981, Fenton's Pat Clark met with Pearl Bedell, who was associated with Wellman Inc., a Boston-based firm, which managed the licensing rights for several designers.

Among those represented by Bedell and Wellman Inc. were a Swedish designer, Katja, and an American husband-wife team, Yale and Frances Forman. Ultimately, Fenton produced two lines of glassware, "Katja/Fenton USA" and "An American Legacy." Although neither line was successful financially, the members of Fenton's third generation generally feel that these efforts gave the company a positive image in the marketplace and were good "learning" experiences.

Katja/Fenton USA

Don Fenton and Pat Clark visited the Katja showroom in New York City in September, 1981. They liked the Katja House concept, and they thought Fenton could make and sell Katja-designed glassware. Katja House was then being marketed in nearly 30 department stores nationwide, including Macy's, Bloomingdale's, Neiman Marcus, and Woodward & Lothrop. The prospect of selling Fenton glass through these outlets was enticing, indeed.

In April, 1982, Katja sent preliminary sketches for several dozen items (ranging from table center bowls and plates plus candlesticks to candy dishes, vases and bud vases). George Fenton discussed Katja's proposed shapes with Bud Ward (Hot Metal foreman) and Carnick Hamperian (Mould Room foreman), and some cost and production difficulties were anticipated. George was confident, however, especially regarding the various vase shapes. Katja revised her design ideas, and Fenton worked on samples. Fenton considered six colors (Seafoam, Heather, Bisque, Blue, Black and Bone White) plus crystal for several vases and bowls in plain shapes. Plates, lamps and an ivy ball were also planned.

Katja and her husband, Rod Geiger, visited the Fenton plant on August 9-10, 1982, and production moved very quickly from that point. Wooden moulds were used for the basic shapes of blown bottles, bowls, cylinders and vases. The number of colors was reduced to four—Blue, Aquamarine, Hickory and Flame—and

each was used (as a band, rim, spiral or fade effect) to accent a crystal piece.

Katja's background was not in glass design, although her father was a well-known sculptor and ceramist in Sweden. She designed both clothing and shoes for the European market, but her reputation in the United States was based upon Saks Fifth Avenue sportswear as well as fabrics (Cannon towels and linens) and wall coverings.

Nancy Fenton recalls that Katja felt "very, very strongly" about the plain shapes of the pieces, but her views on the color bands altered. At first, Katja wanted the bands sharply defined, but she changed her mind when she saw the efforts of Fenton's skilled glassworkers. After the initial gathering of a crystal gob, the worker placed a bit of colored glass in the appropriate place. When the piece is blown to its final shape, the color stretches to create the band or fade effect, but no two pieces are exactly alike.

Making the Katja pieces presented real challenges to

Fenton's Delmer Stowasser works as Katja looks on.

Fenton's workers, and some little-used operations, such as shearing or hot cut-off, had to be renewed and mastered. These articles were stuck up on pontil rods, too, another procedure previously used sparingly. The colored rims on Katja pieces were applied in much the same fashion as used for Fenton's "crest" wares. With practice, the workers quickly became reasonably proficient in all phases of the operation, although there were production problems resulting in low yields.

Fenton developed eight possible trademark or logo markings to be used for the Katja pieces, and renderings were submitted to Katja. All involved combinations of the capital letters "K" and "F" in various typestyles and positions.

Katja/Fenton logo.

Using a rubber-coated brass template, Fenton workers sandblasted the chosen logo on the bottom of each piece.

The Katja items were unveiled at the tabletop show in New York City's Prince George Hotel in November, 1982. This was the first show attended by Nancy Fenton and Shelley Fenton, and they recall the frantic preparations. The samples were not ready to be shipped beforehand, so Nancy and Shelley had to take them on the plane to New York. "We each checked three or four master cartons of glass, and when we went from the airport in New York to the hotel, we had to take two separate taxicabs," Shelley remembers.

Some of the fixtures (large white cubes for the Katja section) and furniture groupings (tables, chairs, and a hutch as well as Capel rugs from North Carolina for the American Legacy display) were not on hand when set-up commenced Saturday morning. A series of telephone calls finally resulted in delivery late Saturday afternoon. Arrangements had to be made to remove the hotel's picture windows so the furniture could be moved into Fenton's display area.

Nancy and Shelley, along with Don Fenton and Pat Clark, finally got to work in the late afternoon on setting up the entire Fenton display (Katja, An American Legacy and the rest of the line). As it happened, Bill Fenton had secured tickets for the popular Broadway play "A Chorus Line," and he had planned for Shelley to attend with him. "I was anxious to get back to help the others," Shelley remembers, "and I returned just after 11." Nancy also recalls the long night of work: "We finished about 6 am, just in time for a quick shower."

A special 12-page Katja catalog was designed and printed in New York City. A press party, funded in part by Fenton, was held at Katja's loft showroom on

Hang-tag for Katja/Fenton items.

November 5, 1982, and some of those attending the tabletop show were invited to visit the showroom during November 7-10. The Katja/Fenton line consisted of 19 different items in four colors: Crystal with Blue (KC); Crystal with Hickory (KN); Crystal with Aquamarine (KE); and Crystal with Flame (KO).

At the tabletop show, there were "ooh's and aah's" from many prominent department store buyers, such as Ted Taylor of Federated Department Stores. The Katja ware was displayed on white cubes at one end of Fenton's display area, while An American Legacy was at the other.

Early reports were positive. At the Annual Stockholders Meeting on February 24, 1983, it was noted that "The Katja designed ware has allowed us to re-enter the department store market...We are excited over the new 'concepts' approach to marketing and the potential we see for additional business." Unfortunately, not enough department store buyers ordered the Katja pieces, and, except for Famous Barr in St. Louis and a few others, most of them had difficulty getting retail customers to buy it.

Retail prices for Katja items ranged from lows of $20 (K7751) and $22.50 (K7761 and K7764) to a high of $49.50 (K7713, K7763 and K7766). By mid-1983, eight items had been discontinued. By the late summer of 1983, Fenton sought to close out the entire Katja line.

Various aspects of competition and marketing also played key roles. Imported ceramics were quite popular at the time Katja glass was introduced, and, in the glass trade, there was a good deal of rather inexpensive, plain glass being imported. Katja may have been "cutting edge," but the clean, contemporary look could be purchased more cheaply elsewhere.

Additionally, the Katja pieces did not fit the traditional view of Fenton glass, and this made it hard to sell. As Nancy Fenton noted, "Buyers had a very definite image of Fenton in their minds, and the Katja pieces were totally inconsistent with that image. Some even thought we were only marketing it, and it was being made in Europe."

Finally, the concept idea did not really take hold in the department stores, although it did work well for the "bed and bath" section. There were well-established buyers for different areas within the stores (gifts, glassware, linens, wall coverings, etc.), and they didn't adapt to the idea of the concept shop.

Katja/Fenton line

K7711	.8³/₄" fruit bowl, banded color
K7713	.12" fruit bowl, banded color
K7722	.7¹/₂" flared bowl, banded color
K7724	.9¹/₂" flared bowl, banded color
K7743	.5¹/₄" cylinder, spiral color
K7744	.8¹/₄" cylinder, spiral color
K7748	.8¹/₄" cylinder, spiral color
K7751	.3¹/₂" vase, fade color
K7752	.5¹/₂" vase, fade color
K7753	.7" vase, fade color
K7754	.3¹/₂" vase, color rim
K7755	.5¹/₂" vase, color rim
K7756	.7" vase, color rim
K7761	.4" bottle, banded color
K7762	.6" bottle, banded color
K7763	.8" bottle, banded color
K7764	.4" bottle, color rim
K7765	.6" bottle, color rim
K7766	.8" bottle color rim

These pieces were made in Crystal with Blue (KC); Crystal with Hickory (KN); Crystal with Aquamarine (KE); and Crystal with Flame (KO).

K 7765 KN

K 7763 KN

K 7762 KN

K 7744 KN

K 7743 KN

K 7761 KN

K 7755 KN

K 7722 KN

or code for Hickory is KN

KATJA™
Fenton, USA

K 7753 KN

K 7751 KN

K 7752 K

Ad for the Katja line.

35

An American Legacy

Another licensing agreement brought Fenton into association with a husband-wife team, Yale and Frances Forman. The Formans already had a reputation as color forecasters, and they were pioneers in the Color Marketing Group, an organization devoted to color trends across various industries. The Formans developed the theme "An American Legacy," and a logo depicting a tall three-masted clipper ship was chosen to reflect the late 18th-early 19th-century Federal Period influence.

**Logo for
An American Legacy**

Most of the Formans' products by 1981-82 were textiles, such as upholstery fabrics and wall coverings. The long-range plans, however, were wide-ranging, as the Formans had designed area rugs, decorative pillows, desk accessories and porcelain china tableware as well as linens for the kitchen, bath and bedroom.

Fenton reasoned that the Federal Period style of An American Legacy would fit naturally with its traditional glassware products. As with Katja, Fenton also wanted to reach department store and finer specialty store buyers, and the Wellman group had played up its previous marketing success with this clientele.

The Formans lacked glass design experience, so they perused Fenton catalogs to develop ideas. Fenton wanted to avoid major expenditures for new moulds, so the Formans were encouraged to adapt existing moulds. The Formans visited Fenton in May, 1982, and the Gift Shop introduced them to the current line. In the Fenton Museum, the Formans studied a wide variety of Fenton's past efforts.

After the Formans' visit to the mould room and a discussion of mould shapes, it was time for lunch. Bill Fenton had a previous commitment, so Pat Clark quickly looked about for someone to add to the luncheon party. Quite by chance, Nancy Fenton (who was then working part-time) was invited to join the group. "We just had a wonderful time," Nancy recalls. "We spoke the same color language and were interested in the same things."

Fenton's and the Formans' efforts were pointed toward the introduction of glassware for An American Legacy at the November tabletop show in New York City. The focus was on relatively plain items with an optic pattern, and three colors were chosen for initial production—Amethyst (AY), Federal Blue (FB) and a canary-yellow hue called "Candleglow" (YL).

An American Legacy by Fenton

G1603	sugar and cream set
G1606	salt and pepper set
G1618	8" oval relish
G1625	11" oval bowl
G1632	4¹/₂" vase
G1636	7" basket
G1644	5 oz. wine
G1645	10 oz. goblet
G1652	10" vase
G1659	7" vase
G1660	70 oz. pitcher
G1661	small pitcher
G1665	6" bell
G1674	cruet w/stopper
G1678	decanter w/stopper
G1692	sugar shaker
G9071	candlesticks

These items were made in four colors: Amethyst (AY),
Federal Blue (FB), Heritage Green (HG),
and Candleglow (YL).

Some moulds had been used recently for Fenton's "Sculptured Ice Optics" pieces. The rib optic effect in An American Legacy was quite different, however, resembling the so-called "pillar-moulded" articles of the early 1800s.

Fenton introduced An American Legacy at the annual November show in New York City (the Katja line made its debut at the same time). An illustrated booklet profiled the Formans ["well known and respected in the home furnishings industry for their work in color forecasting as well as design"] and described the glassware shapes ["accurately reflects the discrete elegance of the Federal Period"].

Fenton's American Legacy colors were planned to match fabrics developed by the Formans, and the booklet showed samples to reinforce this notion. The association with Fenton was the Formans' first venture with glass, and they were generally more concerned with matching colors rather than with complementing colors. Although this was a trend in home furnishings at the time (and Fenton sought to tie into it), Nancy Fenton feels, in

Frances and Yale Forman

An American Legacy

FROM

Fenton

G1644 5 oz. wine and G1645 10 oz. goblet.

retrospect, that more emphasis upon color coordination might have been beneficial to the American Legacy idea. For example, cranberry glass might have made a nice complement to a printed fabric with yellow background rather than producing yellow glass.

In response to requests from Fenton sales representatives, a 5 oz. wine (G1644) and a 10 oz. goblet (G1645) were added to the American Legacy series in 1983. This stemware was difficult to make, however, and Fenton had to compete with cheaper, machine-made stemware. Nancy Fenton recalled that "the first ones were great" but later production "had problems with settle waves." The 7" basket (G1636) in Federal Blue proved to be a reason-

ably good seller when it was added to the American Legacy group (plans for other items were shelved due to the costs of making moulds and the general sales performance of the American Legacy line as well as the worsening financial situation at Fenton).

In December, 1982, however, Fenton had reason for optimism regarding the American Legacy collection. Several department stores (Hecht Co., M. O'Neil Co. and Bon Ton) had placed good orders, and Fenton had favorable responses from two major mail order catalogues, Spiegel and Sturbridge Yankee Workshop.

By mid-1983, the American Legacy pieces were available in a fourth color, Heritage Green (HG). The Formans were working on fabrics in a grey-tone green, and Fenton's Heritage Green matched well. Sales of American Legacy in 1983 were reasonably steady, but some popular items, such as the pitcher and candlesticks, were difficult to produce consistently.

When Yale and Frances Forman visited Fenton in January, 1984, to review the American Legacy program, the line had been cut back in Candleglow (nine items) and Amethyst (five items). Fenton had just introduced the Dusty Rose (DK) color, and there was some discussion of making American Legacy pieces. As it turned out, Heritage Green was dropped in June, 1984, and no Dusty Rose items were added. Federal Blue proved to be the best-selling American Legacy color, and the candlesticks, the basket, the handled pitcher and the bell were the most popular items.

✳ ✳ ✳ ✳ ✳ ✳

Although the Katja and American Legacy groupings were not strong sellers, they did focus Fenton's attention on market-driven design considerations and on the development of skills among glassworkers. In the long run, both of these lessons were expensive but valuable.

The Sculptured Rose Quartz 9" Lady vase (7661 LJ) was made for the first Connoisseur Collection in 1983.

As Fenton glass grew increasingly popular among collectors, the company developed more "collectible" products. Many were limited editions, and Fenton artists or designers were often associated with particular items. Some were intended for special occasions, such as Mother's Day, Easter or Christmas (see Chapter Twenty-One). The most extensive grouping in the 1980s was the "Connoisseur Collection," which was launched in mid-1983.

The announcement of the Connoisseur Collection reflects both Frank Fenton's influence and much of the company's rationale: "With the guidance of Frank M. Fenton, Chairman and connoisseur of fine American Glass, we have put together this group of nine items as a very special offering for those who love glass and desire the unique." Bottom-line profit was not of paramount concern, as the company sought to create prestigious glassware products. Relatively few articles were made, and most have turned out to be real "bargains," especially when one views prices in the secondary market years later.

Between 1983 and 1990, Fenton offered sixty Connoisseur Collection pieces. For the most part, these reflect the look of "old" art glass and allowed the company to refine design ideas and glassmaking techniques. Ten new articles were offered in 1986 and in 1990, while just five debuted in 1988 and only two in 1987. The retail

prices for Connoisseur items ranged from a low of $25.00 (9660 WI in 1983 and 9163 UR in 1984) to $300 or more (7602 EB in 1985 and 7400 SB in 1986). Most were in the $50.00-95.00 range and came with individual gift boxes and certificates of authenticity.

Connoisseur Collection pieces were typically offered as numbered, limited editions. Although the catalog supplements provide the numerical limits, collectors should bear in mind that the quantity of items actually made and sold was often lower than the limits, especially when an article was difficult to produce because problems were encountered in Hot Metal. Among the best-selling items were the 7661 LJ Lady vase (1983), the 9458 AV 8" Embossed Swan vase (1984), and the 8808 SB decorated Burmese vase (1985).

The Connoisseur Collection sometimes spotlighted Fenton's popular and collectible glasses (such as Burmese, Blue Burmese, and various Cranberry effects), and it also revived earlier wares (such as Plated Amberina and Vasa Murrhina). Most of all, however, the Connoisseur Collection strived for the unique, embracing a wide range of interesting hot metal effects and cold metal treatments—from cased glass, iridized glass or heat-sensitive glass to handpainted decorations or elaborate sandcarving.

The initial Connoisseur Collection in 1983 had two articles in pressed Burmese (7562 UF handpainted bell and 7605 BR epergne); some 2000 bells were made, but the epergne was limited to just 500, one of the smallest quantities ever available in the entire history of the collection. The handpainted floral motif on the bell was designed by decorator Linda Everson. Two items were made in Vasa Murrhina: 6432 IM 9" basket and 6462 IM 7^1/$_2$" cruet (each limited to 1000). Two iridized pieces were produced, both in White Satin Carnival glass, the 9640 WI Craftsman Stein (limited to 1500) and the 9660 WI Craftsman Bell (limited to 3500). These Craftsman moulds date from the 1970s, and the pieces depict skilled glassworkers at their jobs.

The remaining three items in the 1983 Connoisseur Collection were "Sculptured Rose Quartz." These were sandcarved pieces, and the Catalog Supplement described them as "a new treatment in glass for Fenton" noting that "the sculptor carves away the rose in layers to provide the shading and tones in each design." Sculptured Rose Quartz is described as "blue-gray on the inside, deep rose on the surface."

Two of these pieces, the 7661 LJ 9" Lady vase (limited to 850) and the 7659 GJ 7" vase (limited to 1500), were based upon designs by sandcarving pioneer Michael Yates, who had a flourishing business in Cleveland. The third Sculptured Rose Quartz piece (7542 FJ 4^1/$_2$" oval vase) was designed by Fenton's Richard Delaney and limited to 2000 pieces. Fenton's 7661 LJ Lady vase was recognized by the Society of Glass and Ceramic Decorators as the winner of its 1983 Discovery Award.

The Connoisseur Collection for 1984 consisted of eight pieces. Three (3193 PV 6" x 8" Top Hat and 5090 PV Cane, ltd. 1500; and 3134 PV 10" Basket, ltd. 1250) were Fenton's Plated Amberina Velvet (PV), based on an old

These Vasa Murrhina items (6432 IM 9" basket and 6462 IM cruet) were made for the first Connoisseur Collection in 1983.

Libbey treatment. Fenton, however, used three layers—opal, ruby and crystal. Fenton made Plated Amberina (PA) in 1962, and some pieces were satin-finished at that time (see *Fenton 3*, p. 77, fig. 204).

Rose Velvet, described as Fenton's "new color," was available in two vases with different treatments. The 7661 MD 9" Mother & Child Vase was decorated by "hand carving, etching and polishing" (the Society of Glass and Ceramic Decorators cited this vase for "excellence in technique" in 1984). Fenton's 9651 HD 9" hand-painted vase was created by Linda Everson, and the floral motif was described as "a soft, almost oriental effect." Each vase was limited to 750.

The Gold Azure (AV) 9458 8" Embossed Swan Vase (limited to 1500) featured opal glass covered with azure blue accented by vivid gold iridescence inside the elaborately crimped top. The iridescent treatment was obtained by spraying in Hot Metal. After the pieces came through the lehr, specially-ordered balloons were stretched over the crimped top and pulled part way down the neck. The balloons protected these areas while the rest of the piece was acid-etched and polished to achieve the desired effect.

The Blue Burmese (UE) 9394 three-piece covered Candy Box (ltd. 1250) was described as "subtle gray-blue which becomes pink when reheated on the outer edges." The final item in the 1984 Connoisseur Collection was the 9163 Ruby Satin Iridescent (UR) Famous

Women Bell, which was limited to 3500. The bell depicts three noteworthy American women—Saint Elizabeth Ann Seton, Helen Keller and Amelia Earhart.

For the centennial anniversary of Frederick S. Shirley's Burmese glass in 1985, Fenton created four pieces of decorated Burmese for its Connoisseur Collection. Three (7602 22" Lamp, ltd. 350; 7666 6½" Bell, ltd. 2500; and 7634 8½" high Basket, ltd. 1250) featured the handpainted decoration Butterfly and Flowering Branch (EB) created by Linda Everson. The fourth, an off-hand vase made by glassworker Delmer Stowasser, was decorated with a handpainted shell motif created by Dianna Barbour. Designated the "8808 SB Shell Vase," only 950 of these were to be made.

The 6602 LY Gabrielle Sculptured French Blue 12" oval vase (ltd. 800) was inspired by Alphonse Marie Mucha's "Musique," and each was sandcarved by Fenton's Bernard Richards. The 8806 GC 7½" vase (ltd. 1000) featured an acid-etched satin finish accented by handpainted chrysanthemums designed by Linda Everson.

Green opalescent glass, first made by Fenton about 1907, was revived for the 3712 GO 14 pc. Punch Set (ltd. 500 sets) and the 4809 GO 4 pc. Diamond Lace Epergne Set (ltd. 1000). A crystal ladle (9975 CY) was available separately for the punch set, which consisted of bowl, base and a dozen cups. The Diamond Lace epergne was first in the Fenton line about 1948, having been designed by Frank L. Fenton based on the c. 1887 Vesta pattern made by the Aetna Glass and Manufacturing Company .

The 1986 Connoisseur Collection consisted of ten articles. Cranberry opalescent glass was lightly iridized to create Cranberry Pearl (CZ) and acid-etched to make French Cranberry Satin (ZS). Two items were made in Cranberry Pearl (7802 10" Boudoir Lamp, ltd. 750; and 7863 Cruet, ltd. 1000), and one piece was made in French Cranberry Satin (3194 13" two-handled urn, ltd. 1000). A similar but smaller double-handled vase, designated 3190, was made in French Royale (KF); these were limited to 1000. The 3104 BI vanity set (ltd. 1000) combined two Blue Ridge perfume bottles with a French Royale puff box on a French Opalescent tray.

Dianna Barbour extended her popular handpainted Shells on Burmese (SB) motif with two items, the 7400 Mariner Lamp (ltd. 1000) and the 7666 Bell (ltd. 2500). Richard Delaney adapted Victor Lhuer's c. 1913 "Danielle" for the sandcarved 8812 10½" Vase in Teal Overlay (JY), and this same color was used for the 7438 Top Hat Basket decorated with handpainted red roses (JD). The vase was limited to 1000, and the basket was limited to 1500. Linda Everson's handpainted Misty Morning decoration was featured on the 8812 10½" Vase (ET), and production was limited to 1000. Her inspiration for Misty Morning came from a Rookwood pottery vase.

In 1987, just two articles formed the Connoisseur Collection. Both were decorated items, and both were limited to 950 pieces. Dianna Barbour was responsible for the 1796 Cranberry Blossoms and Bows Vase (BY). The 9468 Enameled Azure Pitcher (QY), which was designed by Linda Everson, is reminiscent of the vase made by Fenton in 1984 for Avon's Gallery Originals Collection.

The Connoisseur Collection for 1988 was composed of five items, and the stated limits for these ranged from 2000 to 4000, quite a bit higher than earlier Connoisseur Collection offerings. Fenton's sales experience in previous years suggested that the marketplace (both Fenton dealers and subsequent retail customers) could absorb more pieces.

Linda Everson designed the decorations for both the 6080 Wave Crest cranberry candy box (ZX; ltd. 2000) and the 7666 bell in Wisteria (ZW; ltd. 4000). The 2065 ZC pitcher (ltd. 3500) and 2556 ZI vase (ltd. 3500) featured an outer layer of opalescent glass and a teal edge; the vase was also iridized. The 3132 OT basket (ltd. 2500) combines a teal interior with Vasa Murrhina and an iridescent treatment.

The Connoisseur Collection for 1989 featured five items made from Fenton's Rosalene (RE) glass. Three items in Rosalene—7605 5 pc. Epergne (ltd. 2000); 8354 Basketweave Vase (ltd. 2500); and 7060 Diamond Pitcher (ltd. 2500)—were complemented by two handpainted articles in Rosalene Satin—9308 TT 21" Classic Student

Linda Everson

Fenton decorator Linda Everson was responsible for many designs for handpainted decorations on Connoisseur Collection pieces. She first joined Fenton in July, 1968, shortly after Louise Piper had arrived from the Jeannette Shade and Novelty firm in Pennsylvania to start Fenton's Decorating Department. Linda had done oil-painting as a hobby, and she won many county fair awards while in grade school. She quickly learned to paint the Violets in the Snow decoration and others, but Linda left Fenton in 1970 to care for her young family. She came back for a four-month stint in September, 1975, "to help out with Christmas orders" and then returned to Fenton full-time in 1978, when the Decorating Department was a very busy place indeed.

In 1980, Linda became a designer and trainer. In 1985, she became a "working foreman" (still represented by AFGWU local 508), helping with supervision and the training of new decorators and serving on the Fenton design committee which worked on decorations. Linda submitted design ideas, and the first to appear in the Fenton line was the handpainted Strawberries on French Opalescent (SF), which debuted in the 1981-1982 catalog. It moved well, and additional items were soon added.

During the 1980s, Linda developed other designs—Dianthus on Custard (DN), Frosted Asters on Blue (FA), Berries and Blossoms (RK), Copper Rose (KP) and Antique Rose (AF)—and she was also involved with articles for the Childhood Treasures series and the Artists' Series as well as Mother's Day pieces and many items in the Connoisseur Collection. Linda also did the art work for the "anniversary" decal items. In May, 1990, she chose to return to the production area in Fenton's Decorating Department.

Linda enjoyed submitting designs, but she also recalls the tough times in the 1980s: "We had to really scratch to get the product out there...This is giftware, so you really had to appeal in a special way." She derived many good feelings from "creating and being satisfied with myself that the design was right," but her greatest satisfactions come from developing popular designs which generated sales and allowed the Decorating Department to prosper: "I was doing my job to help the decorators keep their jobs!"

Linda recalls the positive climate of the committees which worked on new products: "We all worked together to make the product...It helped a lot when Nancy came in and she started coordinating things...[and] helping with a lot of the ideas...We didn't link our decorating patterns with the color of glass at the time. When I did the raspberries [Berries and Blossoms], I linked up the color I blushed on the tops with the DK color we were making in Hot Metal." She also underscores Fenton's growing emphasis on understanding its market and the customer: "We would find out what was needed out there and then make it."

Married 37 years, Linda and her husband Dorsey have three grown children and three grandchildren.

Delmer Stowasser

Skilled glassworker Delmer Stowasser, who made articles off-hand and was a blow shop finisher, was involved with several Connoisseur Collection pieces as well as other important Fenton products. He worked at Fenton for a quarter-century before retiring in 1990.

Delmer began his career as a carrying-in boy at the Blenko Glass Co. in Milton, West Virginia. In 1946, he was employed at the Bischoff Glass Co. in Cullodon, West Virginia. He carried-in and worked behind the lehrs before learning to gather glass. After serving with the U. S. Army (he was awarded the Bronze Star) in the Korean War, Delmer returned to Bischoff and became a finisher in the tableware plant. He was a handler and foot-setter, and he made various candle holders with twisted stems or air-trap stems. When the Bischoff firm was purchased by the Indiana Glass Company, Delmer

considered relocating his family to Dunkirk, Indiana, but a friend employed at Fenton urged him to apply there in 1965.

In 1974-75, Delmer worked closely with Robert Barber, who created several off hand articles which became a special Fenton line. Frank and Bill Fenton often suggested that Delmer work somewhat independently with hot glass techniques and off hand items, and they saw to it that he had the needed "helpers" to encourage this sort of experimentation. In 1980, Delmer made these off hand items in crystal or milk glass with colored frit to produce various vasa murrhina effects: 5009 egg; 5010 mushroom; 5011 bird; 5012 elephant; 5013 whale; and 5014 penguin. "I spent several months on those animals," Delmer recalled, "and that elephant was fun to make."

Many of the Katja line items were made by blow shops with Delmer as finisher, and he enjoyed working with the different colors to produce the fade effects. "The blue was different from that orange," he noted, "and it took us several weeks to learn how to work the colors." In 1983, Delmer created off-hand "apples" in some of Fenton's overlay colors. Bill Fenton liked the apples so well that they soon went into the regular Fenton line and were featured on the front cover of the January, 1984, catalog supplement.

Artist Dan Dailey worked closely with Delmer, too, and he is especially proud of an off hand vase for Dailey that was featured on the cover of *Glass in Design* for Winter/Spring, 1985. When Nancy Fenton began working with the ideas that resulted in Fenton's Masterworks Collection, she enlisted Delmer's assistance and expertise. She was interested in cased glass vases with an applied dot and threads. After several weeks of trials, he worked out a way to apply the colored threads using a hand-held propane torch to fuse the thin rods to the surface of the vase. "It was a challenge," Delmer remembers, "and you needed steady hands and lots of concentration to do it right."

The Masterworks Collection vases were initially shaped off hand after the colored core was covered with milk glass or another opaque color. "I used wet newspaper that was soaked in water overnight," Delmer related, "and, believe it or not, I found that some newspapers worked better than others. The Parkersburg and the Columbus papers were pretty good, but the Marietta paper wasn't." A tilted marver was used in shaping the triangular 8803 vase.

"That dot was another problem," Delmer recalled. "It was supposed to be round, but a lot of them came out sort of oblong because the vases weren't big enough when blown into the mould. I tried to get my vases just right before putting that dot on."

In 1984, Delmer made the 5090 cane in Plated Amberina to go with the Connoisseur Collection's 3193 Top Hat. For the 1985 Connoisseur Collection, he made all of the 8808 vases in Fenton's Burmese glass. These were blown completely off hand, and, after the piece was stuck-up, the top was carefully hand-shaped and re-heated in a glory hole to strike the salmon pink color.

Lamp (ltd. 1000) and 9667 KT bell (ltd. 3500), both of which were designed by Linda Everson.

Linda Everson also created handpainted decorations for both the 1330 bubble optic Basket in Cranberry with crystal edge (TE; ltd. 2500) and the 2085 drapery optic covered candy box in Cranberry (TM; ltd. 2500). The 6453 Vasa Murrhina (RG) 8" pinch vase (ltd. 2000) was a revival of a glassmaking technique used at Fenton in the mid-1960s. This vase is made with two layers—opal and crystal—but the distinctive colors are created by chips of aventurine green and ruby which are trapped in between.

The 1990 Connoisseur Collection was billed as the "85th Anniversary Offering," and all ten articles were Burmese with handpainted decorations. These were not limited to specific production numbers but were restricted to "May through November Sales," as noted in Fenton's June 1990, Catalog Supplement.

Linda Everson designed both Petite Floral (QJ) and Raspberry Burmese (QH). The former appeared on the 7202 QJ epergne and 7701 QJ cruet with stopper, while the latter graced these: 7731 QH 7" basket; 7412 QH 21" student lamp; and 7700 QH 7-pc. water set.

Two of Louise Piper's earlier designs were adapted for pieces in the 1990 offering. Frances Burton was responsible for the Trees Scene (QD) on the 7792 9" vase and 7732 5¹⁄₂" basket, while Dianna Barbour worked with Rose Burmese (RB), which appeared on these: 7791 6¹⁄₂" vase; 7790 6" vase with fan top; and 9308 20" classic lamp (for Piper's Scenic Decorated and Rose Burmese, see *Fenton 3*, p. 81).

In the 1990s, Fenton continued to develop the Connoisseur Series as a showcase for its very best glassmaking efforts. New colors and innovative treatments were seen, and Fenton's Frances Burton and Martha Reynolds created many handpainted decorations. Ⓕ

Although the Connoisseur Collection may be the best known of Fenton's collectibles from the 1980s, other "series" collectibles are important. These range from collector's plates (including Christmas plates) and decorated items for special occasions (Mother's Day and Christmas) to articles devoted to a theme, such as American Classics, Childhood Treasures or Birds of Winter. The 1980s also saw Fenton create its Designer Series (1983-1986) and Artists' Series (1982-1989), both featuring handpainted scenes on satin-finished opaque colors. For the most part, Fenton's series collectibles were an outgrowth of the strong collector interest in special plates in the 1970s.

At the beginning of the 1980s, Fenton was nearing the conclusion of two long-running offerings of collector plates. Both had begun in 1970, although the Craftsman Series preceded the Christmas in America series by about six months (see *Fenton 3*, pp. 40-41). The Craftsman Series began with the Glassmaker in 1970, and the Tanner and Housewright plates concluded the series in 1980 and 1981, respectively. Except for the

1981, depicted the mission of San Xavier del Bac in Tucson, Arizona. All twelve plates were made in Fenton's amethyst Carnival (CN), White Satin (WS) and Blue Satin (BA); *Fenton 3* erroneously reports that the plates were made in Blue Marble. The final plate, San Xavier del Bac (1981) was also made with the Florentine decoration (FL), handpainted and signed by the artist. At $25.00, this decorated version was the most expensive plate of the entire series (the 1980 plates were $16.50, and the other 1981 plates were $18.50).

Craftsman Series Plates

Housewright ....(1981)
Tanner ....(1980)
Cabinetmaker ....(1979)
Wheelwright ....(1978)
Potter ....(1977)
Gunsmith ....(1976)
Silversmith-Paul Revere ....(1975)
Cooper-John Alden ....(1974)
Shoemaker ....(1973)
Blacksmith ....(1972)
Printer ....(1971)
Glassmaker ....(1970)

These Fenton plates were made in amethyst Carnival (CN) glass.

Christmas in America Series Plates

San Xavier del Bac ....(1981)
Christ Church ....(1980)
San Jose y Miguel de Aguayo ....(1979)
The Church of the Holy Trinity ....(1978)
San Carlos Borromeo de Carmelo ......(1977)
The Old North Church ....(1976)
Birthplace of Liberty ....(1975)
The Nation's Church ....(1974)
St. Mary's in the Mountains ....(1973)
The Two Horned Church ....(1972)
The Old Brick Church ....(1971)
The Little Brown Church in the Vale ....(1970)

These plates were made in amethyst Carnival (CN) glass, White Satin (WS) and Blue Satin (BA).

Glassmaker, all of these plates were designed by Fenton's Tony Rosena. All were made in amethyst Carnival glass (CN) only (although the Glassmaker plate was sampled in milk glass), and the moulds were destroyed at the end of each issue year.

The Christmas in America series depicted historic church buildings. The first (1970) was The Little Brown Church in the Vale, and in 1980, the featured religious establishment was Christ Church in Alexandria, Virginia. The final plate in the series, intended for Christmas,

Mother's Day Series

Fenton was successful with Tony Rosena's Mother's Day plates in the 1970s, so the firm continued to produce appropriate gift items for this special occasion. In the 1980s, Linda Everson created six animal-oriented decorations on Custard Satin pieces (7418 8" plate and 7564 6" bell). These carry the phrase "Mother's Day" in cursive writing, followed by the year of issue.

New Born (NB), which depicted a young bird, was the motif for 1980, and Fenton outlets were limited to ordering four plates and six bells each. For the next five issues, orders were accepted from early January until late May or early June. Gentle Fawn (FN) was the motif for 1981, followed by a baby rabbit called Nature's Awakening (NA) for 1982 and Where's Mom (RQ), a cartoon-like raccoon peering over a log, in 1983.

Precious Panda (PM) was the motif for 1984, and the plate and bell were shown with a decorated Panda figurine (5151 PJ) in Fenton's January, 1984, Catalog Supplement (the 5151 bear cub later became the strong-selling Birthstone Bear). Linda Everson's 1985 creation

Where's Mom 7564 RQ bell and 7418 RQ 8" plate.

Precious Panda 7418 PM 8" plate and 7564 PM bell.

for the final issue of this series was Mother's Little Lamb (LA), which depicted a lamb and a butterfly.

In addition to the series discussed above, Fenton made other items which were marketed as Mother's Day gifts. These ranged from decorated bud vases in 1979-80 (9056 TW and 9056 RC) and 4, 6, or 8-piece assortments of decorated petite bells ("Mom," "Mother" and "Grandmother") to a new item, the 7669 musical bell with a pad printed "special day" verse [these were later available in an assortment of Musical Sentiment bells]. Gift-giving items, such as the 5100 Praying Boy and Girl and the Artist Series Flying Geese, were shown on the Mother's Day page in Fenton's catalog, and articles like the Glass Pets and Natural Animals were often nearby, too.

A new Mother's Day series debuted in 1990 with Linda Everson's Mother Swan (SN) plate (7418), bell (7668) and musical bell (7669).

Christmas Series Items

In addition to the Christmas in America plates, Fenton produced other collectible sets for this significant holiday. Some (Christmas Classics Series, 1978-1982) were simply dated with the appropriate year, while others (Christmas Fantasy Series, 1983-1987) limited in quantity. Several Fenton designers—Kay Cunningham, Michael Dickinson, Linda Everson, Diane Johnson and Robin Spindler—were responsible for various motifs, but Diane Johnson created most of them.

Michael Dickinson developed Christmas Morn (CV), which, in 1978, was the first of the five-part Christmas Classics Series. Three items were made in Opal Satin with the Christmas Morn decoration: 7204 colonial lamp; 7300 fairy light; and 7466 bell. Kay Cunningham's Nature's Christmas (NC) decoration was offered in 1979 on the same three articles plus the 7418 8" plate, all in Custard Satin. Diane Johnson's Going Home (GH), also made in Custard Satin, was available on these four articles in 1980.

For 1981, Diane developed All is Calm (AC), a country road and church scene handpainted on Custard Satin; this was featured on the front of Fenton's June, 1981, Catalog Supplement. The 7510 20" student lamp was

available, as were these items: 7204 colonial lamp; 7300 fairy light; 7466 bell; and 7418 8" plate. Robin Spindler created the last of the Christmas Classics Series decorations, Country Christmas (OC), for 1982. It was used on the same five items in Custard Satin.

A result of decoration design contests, Fenton's Christmas Fantasy Series debuted in 1983 with Diane Johnson's Anticipation (AI), depicting two children watching for Santa's arrival at a window. Three items, limited to 7500 each, were done on Custard Satin: 7300 fairy light; 7418 8" plate; and 7667 bell. For 1984, Diane created Expectation (GE), showing a child awaiting Santa at a fireplace. This decoration was done on the same three pieces (but in Opal Satin), plus the 7512 10½" hurricane lamp, the only time this article appeared in the series.

The final two Christmas Fantasy Series items were Diane Johnson's Heart's Desire (WP) and Linda

All is Calm 7300 AC fairy light.

Diane Johnson

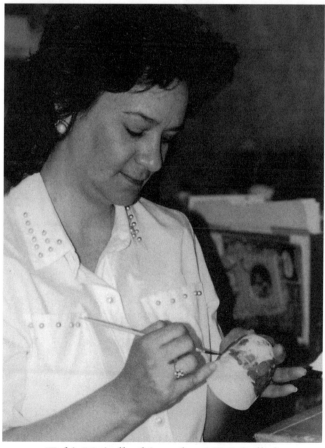

"Robin" Spindler (signs glass J. K. Spindler)

Country Christmas 7204 OC colonial lamp.

Michael Dickinson

Fenton made the 8415 Old Homestead in Winter plate in Cobalt Marigold Carnival glass (NK) for a limited edition of 3500 in 1984.

American Classic Series

The short-lived American Classic Series consisted of two handpainted designs by Michael Dickinson—Jupiter and Studebaker—both executed on Opal Satin glass. Fenton had success with several of Michael's creations in the 1970s, such as the limited edition Mountain Scene and Desert Scene lamps.

In Fenton's 1986-87 catalog, the Jupiter and Studebaker were described as "limited offerings that discriminating collectors will recognize as an opportunity to buy at issue prices." The issue prices were $295 for the Jupiter lamp and $235 for the Studebaker lamp, and the other pieces ranged from $50 to $75.

The Jupiter (TP) depicts "Central Pacific's Jupiter, steaming to the historic joining of East and West by rail at Promontory, Utah, May 10, 1869." The 23" 7514 student lamp was limited to 1000, and the four other pieces (7418 8" plate, 7418 6½" bell, 7698 desk plaque and 8600 clock) were limited to 5000 each.

Everson's Sharing the Spirit (CV). Heart's Desire, which spanned both 1985 and 1986, was done on Custard Satin, and three pieces were offered in a limited edition of 7500 each: 7300 fairy light; 7418 8" plate; and 7667 bell. In March, 1987, Sharing the Spirit was announced via a letter from Don Fenton to Fenton dealers. The same three items were decorated (on Opal Satin glass), but Sharing the Spirit was limited to orders placed by May 15, rather than by a pre-established number.

Some other winter-oriented products bear mention here, namely, the Currier and Ives plates, which were introduced as a four-plate, limited edition "Collection Series" in Fenton's 1981-1982 catalog. The first, entitled Winter in the Country—The Old Grist Mill (8418), was made in Crystal Velvet (VE) as well as Opal Satin decorated with Antique Blue (TB) or Antique Brown (TN). The Old Grist Mill motif was also depicted on a fairy light/vase (8409) and a bell (8461); these were available in Antique Blue, Antique Brown and Crystal Velvet.

The Currier and Ives 8417 Harvest plate appears in the June, 1981, Catalog Supplement, and was available in Antique Blue, Antique Brown and Crystal Velvet as well as a special order in Antique White (WS). The Old Homestead in Winter (8415) plate and the Winter Pastime (8414) plate were introduced in 1982 and 1983, respectively, and these were available only in Antique Blue and Antique Brown. After the series concluded,

Dianna Barbour

Beverly Cumberledge

The other American Classic offering (SU) depicted a c. 1910 Studebaker-Garford parked near a brick building. The 7204 colonial lamp was limited to 1000, and the four other pieces (7418 8" plate, 7418 6½" bell, 7698 desk plaque and 8600 clock) were limited to 5000 of each.

Childhood Treasures Series

This series, variously promoted as a five-issue series and later as a ten-issue series, actually ran for seven years! It consisted of Custard Satin pieces (1760 4½" bell and 7615 3¼" cup plate) with various handpainted decorations created by Fenton decorators. Diane Johnson designed the first in 1983, Teddy Bear (TE). Linda Everson was responsible for the next three years: Hobby Horse (HQ) in 1984; Clown (CL) in 1985; and Playful Kitten (KD) in 1986. Dianna Barbour developed Frisky Pup (PN) for 1987. These five designs were limited to 15,000 bells and 15,000 cup plates each.

The final two Childhood Treasures selections were limited to 5,000 bells and 5,000 cup plates each. Generally speaking, buyer interest in a series tended to be at its peak for the first several issues; from the fourth issue on, enthusiasm tended to wane. For 1988, Dianna Barbour created Castles in the Air (CH), and, in 1989, Diane Johnson was responsible for the seventh and final scene depicting a rocking chair and stuffed animal; this was called A Child's Cuddly Friend (CX).

Designer Series

The short-lived Designer Series (1983-1986) featured handpainted scenic motifs on opaque satin glass and was generally confined to lamps, plates (7418 or 7618) and bells (7466, 7667 or 7668), although a clock (8600) appeared during one year. Michael Dickinson was responsible for three Designer Series motifs, and Susan Bryan, Beverly Cumberledge and Gloria Finn contributed the others.

The first Designer Series pieces, all on Custard Satin, appeared in the June, 1983, Catalog Supplement. The Lighthouse Point design (LT) was featured on lamp shades painted by Michael himself as well as the 7466 bell and 7418 8" plate, which were done by various Fenton decorators. The bell and plate were limited to 1000 each, and Michael painted 300 lamp shades (available on either the 7503 23½" Rochester student lamp or the 7507 25½" French Provincial lamp). Some shades were also used for the 7505 LT swag lamp.

The Down Home design (FV), which was sometimes called "Farm View," was the creation of Gloria Finn, who had worked at Fenton since 1978. The same bell and plate moulds (1000 of each) were used for this Midwestern farm motif, but the 300 lamp shades painted by Gloria were available only with the 7209 21" student lamp.

The 1984 offerings were Beverly Cumberledge's Majestic Flight (EE) and Michael Dickinson's Smoke 'n Cinders (TL), both of which were done on Opal Satin. The bells (7667) and plates (7618) were limited to 1250

Susan Bryan

each. Beverly's "graceful soaring eagle" was available on two lamps (7204 16" colonial and 7503 23½" Rochester, limited to 250 each), while Michael's motif "for train lovers everywhere" was available in the 7514 23" student lamp as well as the 16" colonial style (250 each).

The 1985 Designer Series encompassed three different motifs on Opal Satin by Fenton's designers. Michael Dickinson's In Season (HF) and Beverly Cumberledge's Nature's Grace (DW) were available in two lamps (7204 16" colonial or 7514 23" student; 250 of each) as well as these items, with limits as noted in parentheses: 7618 8" plate (1250); 7667 6" bell (1250); and 8600 clock (2000).

Since 1985 was the 100th anniversary of the Statue of Liberty, Fenton offered several limited edition commemorative items in the Designer Series. Susan Bryan's Statue of Liberty (LO) depicts the famous New York harbor statue on the 7618 8" plate (1250) and the 7668 6" bell (1250). Susan's 1985 design proved to be quite popular, so she prepared another version of the Statue of Liberty (L6), and this close-up portrait appeared in Fenton's 1986-87 Catalog. This was also available on the 7618 8" plate (1250) and the 7668 6" bell (1250).

Artists' Series

Fenton's Artists' Series parallels the Childhood Treasures Series, Both feature handpainted decorations, and both were confined to two articles in Custard Satin (1760 4½" bell and 7615 3¼" cup plate). Both consisted of seven different decorating motifs, and both concluded in 1989, although the inception of the Artists' Series preceded the Childhood Treasures Series by a year.

Diane Johnson designed the first offering in 1982, After the Snow (TC). She was also responsible for Winter Chapel (WC), which was sold during two years (1983-84), as well as Flying Geese (FG) in 1985 and The Hummingbird (HW) in 1986. Linda Everson created Out in the Country (SF), the motif for 1987. Each of these was limited to 15,000 bells and 15,000 cup plates.

The last two Artists' Series decorations—Serenity (AT) in 1988 and Househunting (AC) in 1989—were limited to 5,000 bells and 5,000 cup plates each. Fenton's Frances Burton created Serenity, which depicts a swan, and Dianna Barbour developed the birdhouse for Househunting.

Birds of Winter Series

This limited edition series of four birds depicted in winter scenes ran from 1987 through 1990, spotlighting a different bird each year. Unlike other Fenton series offerings, all the Birds of Winter designs were shown at the outset in the June, 1987, Catalog Supplement. These were developed in conjunction with *Bird Watcher's Digest*, a national magazine printed in nearby Marietta. The first was Cardinal in the Churchyard (BC) in 1987, followed by A Chickadee Ballet (BD) in 1988, Downy Woodpecker—Chiseled Song (BL) in 1989, and A Bluebird in Snowfall (NB) in 1990.

All were designed by Fenton's Diane Johnson and handpainted on Opal Satin glass. Four items were com-

Winter Chapel 1760 WC bell and 7615 WC cup plate

mon to each issue, with limits as noted: 7300 fairy light (4500); 7418 8" plate with stand (4500); 7667 bell (4500); and 8600 clock (1500). Five hundred lamps were made each year, but the styles varied, as follows: Cardinal in the Churchyard (9702 18½" lamp); A Chickadee Ballet (7209 21" student lamp); Downy Woodpecker—Chiseled Song (7204 16" lamp); and A Bluebird in Snowfall (7209 21" student lamp). Four poets associated with *Bird Watcher's Digest* submitted poems for each edition. The selected poems were pad printed on the bells, fairy lights and plates.

In June, 1990, Fenton brought out the Birds of Winter Collector Ornaments. Although not a limited edition, these ornaments, which combined pad printing and handpainting, were "designed to coordinate with the collection of 4 Birds of Winter designs and to cast a spell of rare charm on Christmas." The ornaments (1714 followed by appropriate decoration code) are 3½" in diameter and come furnished with red ribbon loops for ease in hanging on a Christmas tree. The Birds of Winter ornaments were very successful and sold well. The 1714 ornament had been introduced as Pearlized Collector Ornaments in 1989 with four designs then available, as follows: Winter Scene (EA); Dove (EH); Winter Rose (EV); and Skaters (EF).

Interestingly, Fenton had created a "Four Seasons" decorated assortment which depicted birds on the 7466 bell and the 7418 plate in June, 1980. Limited to "experimental sales," these consisted of the following: winter cardinal (FW); spring robin (FR); summer bluebird (FM); and fall brown bird/chickadee (FF). At first, these were sold in sets of four bells ($120-140) or four plates ($140-154) and, later, individually (bells, $35 ea.; plates, $38.50 ea.).

Chapter Twenty-Two
ATTEMPTS AT DIVERSIFICATION

Over the years, Fenton has, from time to time, considered options to diversify the company's interests. In the 1980s, Fenton acted to diversify its efforts in the giftware market by purchasing Thee Bakers Dozen (which was renamed Christine Victoria) and launching two other important ventures—Fenton-From-Afar and the Gracious Touch party plan.

At the time these began (the mid-1980s), the company was in trouble. Its glassware products were not selling well in the competitive giftware marketplace, so Fenton's management—including members of both the second and third generations—decided that the company needed to move in other directions. These efforts also reflect an evolution in the company's design and marketing strategies, namely, a shift from internally-focused design decisions ("design what we like and then sell it to customers") to consumer and market driven approaches ("design to meet consumers' wants and use several channels to reach them").

Although these ventures were not financially successful over the long term, they did have positive effects. Christine Victoria helped Fenton to market its wares to some new department store accounts. More importantly, Christine Victoria re-linked Fenton with many independent gift shops, and the long term results for Fenton glass were favorable.

Christine Victoria

Fenton completed arrangements to acquire a California corporation, Thee Bakers Dozen, in early 1986. Tom Lubbers was involved with Thee Bakers Dozen, and he knew that Fenton was seeking a business to acquire. Thee Bakers Dozen manufactured Victorian-style handmade decorative accessories and accents.

Fenton's management felt that these products (baskets, wall and door decor, and pillows as well as photo albums and Christmas accents) fit well with the Fenton's desire to expand its giftware offerings beyond glass and, furthermore, that Fenton glass could be coordinated with Thee Bakers Dozen lines, which some Fenton reps were already carrying. Fenton also decided to change the name to "Christine Victoria." These terms connoted the Victorian appearance of the product and also were a bit of word play on the previous owners, Christine and Victor Vattuone. Fenton also hoped to tap into new design capabilities.

The efforts of Fenton's reps soon brought in orders. An infusion of new working capital into Christine Victoria to meet this demand and improve manufacturing procedures was necessary. Actual orders exceeded sales projections, however, and the operation expanded very quickly, growing from about a dozen employees to nearly one hundred and moving into larger quarters. Several Fenton executives—George Fenton, Nancy Fenton and Stan Vanlandingham—spent a good deal of time in California. Later, both George and Stan began to institute production management controls on site.

Catalogs were issued by Christine Victoria in 1986-1990, and several of these featured assortments in which Fenton glass was combined with Christine Victoria prod-

ucts. Some Fenton catalog supplements carried out this idea, too. Dusty Rose and Periwinkle Blue were often shown with Christine Victoria items, and Dusty Rose with Victorian Mauve was Fenton's "No. 1 look" in 1986-87.

These assortments renewed interest in Fenton products among the company's independent gift shop accounts and also carried Fenton into new department store accounts. The department store buyers became a factor as Fenton's glass sales began to improve in 1986-87. J. C. Penney stores were very interested in Christine Victoria, particularly in the late 1980s.

The Christine Victoria "Elizabeth Collection" concept encompassed both Fenton glassware and ceramics and accessories which were available from Christine Victoria. This "look" had an impact in the marketplace, and items from the Elizabeth Collection were among Fenton's best sellers in the late 1980s.

The Christine Victoria operation was relocated to Vienna, West Virginia, in 1989 so that Fenton could exert better controls by having the operation close at hand. Christine and Victor Vattuone declined to move, however, and Fenton contracted with Judith Johnson (from Delighted Eye) to assist with design for a time. Later, a management team from Heartland Designs in Missouri was hired. The name was changed slightly to Christine Victoria Designs, Inc.

By 1991, however, it became apparent that crucial cost reductions were not taking place. Sales levelled off and then declined. Some felt that the problems at Christine Victoria Designs were a drain on Fenton management's time and energy at a time when the glass business needed attention. Ultimately, Fenton decided to shut down Christine Victoria Designs as soon as it fulfilled a commitment to supply merchandise to J. C. Penney stores.

Although the Christine Victoria venture was costly, Fenton's management learned from the experience and, in retrospect, most feel that the venture was not without value. Despite the difficulties, Stan Vanlandingham feels that Christine Victoria was instrumental in helping the company build sales volume and re-establish enthusiasm and support for Fenton among the sales reps. Christine Victoria (and Fenton-From-Afar) also gave Fenton a better grasp of the nature of the giftware market.

Fenton-From-Afar

During the summer of 1985, "Fenton-From-Afar" was launched. At the Annual Stockholders Meeting in February, 1985, Fenton's management noted the "continued pressure from imported gift lines" and concluded that "if [we] can't beat them, we may join them by importing a line of giftware ourselves."

An article appeared in "Inside Fenton" (Summer 1985), and a letter to dealer accounts from Bill Fenton (August 1, 1985) accompanied a pocket folder containing full-color sheets showing available items—Wooden Birds, Cloisonne, Brass, Poly Figurines, Jade Porcelain, Ceramic Figurines, and Wooden Jewel Boxes. The cover conveyed a clear message: "Fenton: Your One Source for Quality Giftware." Indeed, George Fenton told those

Front cover of the 1990 Christine Victoria catalog.

Fenton-From-Afar, June, 1987, catalog.

1989-1990

Gracious Touch collection

Front cover of 1989-1990 Gracious Touch brochure.

attending the Annual Stockholders Meeting in early 1986 that Fenton's goal was "to change from a manufacturer of handmade glassware to a supplier of a complete line of giftware."

Fenton-From-Afar catalogs were issued in June, 1986, and June, 1987. Both emphasized an attractive series of handpainted ceramic figurines called "Kith 'N Kin Collectibles." All were available with plain wooden bases, and many could be purchased with musical bases. The Bride and Groom pair played the tune "Endless Love."

The 1987 catalog also featured rattan wreaths and baskets as well as applique pillows. Other Fenton-From-Afar merchandise—such as Plush Huggies (stuffed animals), handpainted bone china, handpainted wooden animal figurines and silk flowers—was featured elsewhere in the catalogs or on color sheets which were mailed to Fenton accounts.

The idea behind Fenton-From-Afar was sound enough, but Fenton ultimately found it impossible to compete with large-volume importers whose contacts in the Far East were better. These firms were able to obtain comparable or higher quality products at more favorable prices, so Fenton decided not to pursue this venture.

Gracious Touch

In the fall of 1986, Fenton launched a "party plan" to sell both Fenton glass and Christine Victoria products. Fenton had experience making private mould and other glassware for other party plans (Princess House, Candle-Land and Tiara), but Gracious Touch brought the company into the party plan business. Fenton signed a contract with a Missouri-based organization, Clevenger and Associates, which was charged with the task of developing this party plan concept.

The idea was simple enough: individuals (usually women working part-time) would become "Sales Associates," hosting in-home parties (to display products and take orders) and recruiting other individuals to host similar parties. Sales Associates earned a commission on sales, and there were also strong incentives to recruit others (called "Demonstrators") into the plan so that Sales Associates could earn bonuses and additional commissions by becoming Sales Advisors or even Sales Directors. The first stage of the effort encompassed ten states plus Washington, D. C., and Clevenger and Associates hoped to attract several hundred Sales Associates within a year or two.

Several brochures and other printed materials show Fenton glassware and Christine Victoria products sold by Gracious Touch in 1986-89. Typically, the Fenton four-digit ware number was preceded by the letter "Q" to designate it as part of the Gracious Touch line. When Fenton reps were told about Gracious Touch in mid-October 1986, Don Fenton assured them that the articles sold would not be in the current Fenton line. Don also noted that party plan sales could ultimately strengthen the retail market as first-time glass buyers in the party plan later sought other Fenton items in giftware stores. The colors used were already in the line or were otherwise scheduled for private mould or Fenton's Antique Trade glass.

More than a dozen Regency pattern articles were made in crystal, and both Hobnail and Lily of the Valley were offered in Sapphire Blue Opalescent (BX). Numerous Lily of the Valley pieces were made in Dusty Rose Velvet (VO), and a heart-shaped dish (Q7333) was produced in Dusty Rose with a Milk Glass "crest" treatment (DM). Other prominent colors were Teal Marigold (OI), Ruby (RU), Country Cranberry (CC), and Teal Crest (UX).

Several handpainted decorations were developed: Peach Roses on opal satin (RP); Pretty Pansies on Custard Satin (PP); and scenic views such as Away in the Manger (N5), Bridge of Love (JG) on Opal Satin and Historic Covered Bridge on Custard Satin (JV). In 1988, a few special pieces for Gracious Touch recruitment awards (Teal Marigold Q9480 Chessie candy box) were signed by Bill, Don or George Fenton.

The 1989-1990 Gracious Touch brochure featured two special items. Fenton's red Carnival glass was revived with the Q8223 RN Orange Tree and Cherry Chain bowl, and a mid-1920s Dolphin two-handled candy box (Q7580 UD) was given new life with an interesting decoration.

The Gracious Touch program started off well, placing many advertisements in the *Glass Review* during 1986-87. Gracious Touch was featured on the magazine's front cover in January, 1987. Several annual conventions were held in Marietta/Williamstown for the Gracious Touch Sales Associates. Ultimately, however, both sales figures and recruitment statistics fell well short of Fenton's goals. Furthermore, Fenton's management was concerned with the costs of printing sales kits and other materials as well as high levels of product inventory without good prospects for sales. Gracious Touch was discontinued in 1990.

✳ ✳ ✳ ✳ ✳ ✳

In retrospect, Fenton's efforts at diversification were costly and difficult, yet valuable experiences. These ventures ran their courses and, one by one, were put aside as demand for Fenton's regular line of glass increased. Fenton's management team had gained important insights into the giftware market and learned that the company's strength and profitability lay in its ability to make and sell glassware. The decision to concentrate on the glass business re-focused everyone's energy as the 1980s drew to a close.

Earlier confined primarily to private mould work, Fenton's Special Products department branched out during the 1980s into new areas—licensed merchandise, college and university-related products, commemorative items, recognition and incentive awards, etc. Both handpainted and decal decorations were used, and sandcarving played an important role in the division's development.

Licensed Merchandise

Fenton acquired the licensing rights to use the logos of Anheuser-Busch and Jack Daniels. Fenton's Pat Clark made presentations to these firms, showing various products as proof of Fenton's workmanship. Sometimes Pat displayed samples with the prospective licensor's logo. This involved getting special masks made and sandcarving done, often on short notice. "That was the secret," Pat noted. "When they saw our quality and their logo together, they were sold." He spent so much time dealing with breweries that Bill Fenton once laughingly asked, "Pat, just <u>who</u> are you working for?"

Among Fenton's first licensed merchandise was a decal rendering of the famous Budweiser Clydesdales, augmented by handpainting to enhance the effect. Nine Clydesdale items appeared in an Anheuser-Busch catalog in 1984 along with sandcarved articles bearing these motifs: Budweiser; Bud Light; Michelob; Michelob Light; Busch; Natural Light; the "A and Eagle"; and "LA." Fenton sold a two-mug package (sandcarved with "This Bud's for You" or "This Bud's for Me") through Kroger's in Marietta, but this idea did not take hold at Anheuser-Busch.

At the height of Spuds Mackenzie's popularity in the mid-1980s, Fenton sandcarved his likeness on nearly 370,000 items, including over 75,000 mugs supplied by the New Jersey-based Durand firm. "We had a semi truck here every six days," Pat Clark recalled. "Most of the finished products went to stores owned by the brewery, but some were available in the Gift Shop." Pat and Richard Delaney developed some new designs incorporating Spuds Mackenzie in Christmas-oriented scenes (coming out of a chimney, driving a sleigh, etc.). The popularity of Spuds Mackenzie among youngsters became his undoing when some adults began to regard his likeness in advertising as objectionable. Sensitive to public pressure, the brewing company scaled back its use of Spuds, and Fenton's "Christmas Spuds" never reached the marketplace, although a few items were closed out in the Gift Shop.

Sandcarved Jack Daniels merchandise proved popular, especially in gift shops at Cracker Barrel restaurants. Linda Frazier, who applies vinyl masks in Fenton's sandcarving department, recalls an order for 10,000 Jack Daniels bottles. "I think I put every one of those masks on," she said. "But I was good at it, and the wage incentives made it worthwhile."

In addition to licensed merchandise, Fenton's Special Products division also did custom work for premiums, recognition awards and business gifts. Don Fenton and Pat Clark displayed Fenton products at a New York City premium show in the early 1980s. The company later got a prime spot near the show entrance by cooperating with the management to allow another exhibitor, Black & Decker, more space.

By the fall of 1983, Fenton was seeking custom sandcarving business. Two ashtrays ($7\frac{1}{2}$" hexagon and a $5\frac{1}{2}$" round; minimum order 100) were available, along with paperweights (round or rectangular), various beverage glasses and a handled, tankard-style mug (minimum order 20 dozen). Lead crystal plates were marketed as plates and as recognition awards with walnut bases. For an order of 100, prices ranged from $17.50 to $21.50 each, depending upon the complexity of the sandcarved design. An April, 1986, price sheet lists more than 40 different articles as blanks for custom sandcarving.

Some especially vivid sandcarved merchandise was made for colleges and universities. This ranged from cobalt blue items for the "Mountaineers" of West Virginia University or the "Pitt Pathers" to ruby articles with silver paint for The Ohio State University (7564 bell, 9056 bud vase, 9042 10 oz. panelled mug, and 4469 ash tray).

Many different organizations sought Fenton sand-

Pat Clark

carved items for various occasions or as special awards. The Reiter Dairy requested a plate depicting a c. 1933 horse drawn milk wagon for its 50th anniversary. Other orders came from L & M Oil Co., Marietta Country Club, Exxon, Forma Scientific, and Borg-Warner, just to mention a few.

Special Orders

Fenton pursued a variety of special products avenues. Many involved sandcarving, but others entailed making a new mould (as for the Kansas Jayhawk figurine) or decorating with pad printing or custom handpainting. In November 1986, for example, Fenton was

Parkersburg Lions bell

offering its 8600 desk clock, gift boxed "with your corporate trademark." These were sandcarved and then decorated with appropriate colors for various firms.

Fenton designer Michael Dickinson did such handpainted decorations as a "Green Toy Tractor" for International Harvester's 5th Annual Toy Show. Michael also created two Marietta Bicentennial pieces—a limited edition (200) lamp based on an oil painting by Sala Bosworth and a plate depicting "The Moundbuilders Earthworks at Marietta in 1788." Four other plates were planned but not issued.

Quite a few colleges and universities ordered handpainted articles, usually to sell to alumni or to give to major donors. Most were Custard Satin lamps depicting various campus scenes, such as buildings or other landmarks, but some wanted plates or bells, too. Among the institutions were these: University of Indiana; University of Iowa; Marietta College; Marshall University; Muskingum College; University of Nebraska; The Ohio State University; and West Virginia University. The order from Ohio State called for the OSU Stadium on Fenton's 7418 plate and a "Mirror Lake" scene on the 7503 student lamp.

Great diversity is found among the custom handpainted decorations from the 1980s. These range from a "Schaller, Iowa, farm scene" on the 7418 Cameo Satin plate to the "IDS Tower" [a 70 story building] in Minneapolis. The cities of Minerva, Ohio, and Batavia, Illinois, ordered items for anniversary years, and the Columbus, Ohio-based organization Ducks Unlimited sought handpainted lamps depicting "Ducks in Flight," while the Parkersburg Homecoming Committee wanted a sternwheeler to carry out its "Back to the River" theme in 1983. Fenton did them all.

Some special products were important fundraising ventures by non-profit organizations. In 1984, the Parkersburg Lions Club had Fenton produce a limited edition (500) sandcarved bell which depicted the Wood County Courthouse. The Lion's president, John Withum, was pictured with Bill Fenton and Pat Clark in a *Parkersburg News* story about the bells (November 22, 1984). Since then, the Lions have had Fenton make many other sandcarved bells depicting historic Parkersburg-area buildings, ranging from the B & O railroad station and various schools to St. Xavier church. The proceeds support the group's efforts in sight conservation and other community projects. Editor's note: Fenton welcomes inquiries from groups interested in developing a fundraising or commemorative program; write to: Don Cunningham, Fenton Art Glass Co., 700 Elizabeth St., Williamstown, WV 26187.

Sometimes, Fenton processed special orders for established accounts which involved decorated glassware. Typically, these were in conjunction with in-store promotions of Fenton glass. In mid-1980, Burnes of Boston ordered handpainted picture frames with Blue Daisies (BD) or Tea Rose (TM). In 1980, O'Neil's of Akron, Ohio, displayed a pansy motif (DP) which had been created by Fenton's Louise Piper. About a year later, she developed a Bird and Holly (GI) on Milk Glass for Gimbel's; this appeared on the 9320 vase and 9462 bell in 1981.

Records in Fenton's Special Products department also document "experimental" or other "special ware." In early 1981, for instance, three new handpainted decorations on Custard Satin glass were being sold on a trial basis: horse and Amish buggy (HX); girl with doll and carriage (PG); and boy with puppy at mailbox (PP). A note from March, 1983, mentions the 5100 VS Praying Boy and Girl (velvet etched SA/salmon transparent glass). These were sold in the Fenton Gift Shop.

Another segment of Fenton's Special Products department involved private mould work. After Art Edwards retired, this area was looked after by Pat Clark, and Shelley Fenton also dealt with a few customers. "That was really something," Shelley remembered, "since I didn't know much about mould work at that time. I was always running to George, Frank or the mould room foreman to ask about making dental bowls or something like that." One such order handled by Shelley was for an 8" dental cuspidor for S. S. White, of Homdel, New Jersey.

In the early 1980s, Fenton made a series of cup plates for Kaleidoscope, a Maryland-based organization run by Paul J. Grassler and Leonard E. Padgett. This limited edition (15,000 sets) series consisted of 13 cup plates in different colors with various "nursery rhyme" themes such as Little Bo-Peep, Humpty Dumpty, Three Little Kittens, Old King Cole and Little Miss Muffet.

Customers had to subscribe for the entire Kaleidoscope series at the outset, buying a dozen plates at $11.95 each including shipping. Plates were to be released about every 8 to 10 weeks beginning in January, 1982. The thirteenth and final plate, Queen of Hearts, "in the famous Fenton Ruby-Amberina" would be free. Each plate was marked with the Fenton oval logo and the Kaleidoscope "Star." Several cup plates

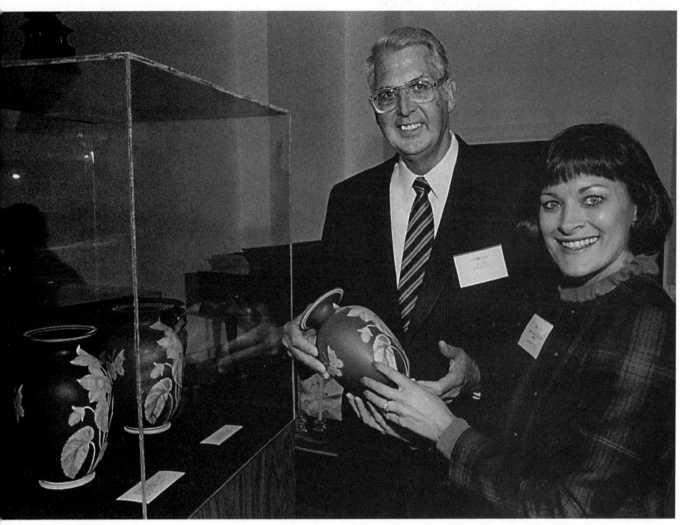

Bill Fenton and Sharon Leonard (Avon's beauty and public relations manager) at the Cincinnati Art Museum.

were difficult to make, and Kaleidoscope did not find it easy to sell the concept of purchasing the entire series. Finally, Bill Fenton arranged for the remaining inventory to be sold through the Fenton Gift Shop.

On October 2, 1984, a Fenton-made vase was unveiled as part of Avon Product's Gallery Originals Collection. A facsimile of an original c. 1880s Stevens and Williams cameo piece from the Cincinnati Art Museum, this splendid azure blue vase was sold through Avon's Gallery Originals catalog, where it was featured on the front cover.

Bill Fenton recalls the initial contact in November, 1983: "Avon had already talked with several other glass companies who told them that Fenton was really the best place to turn. On the phone, Avon purchasing agent Tom Dachik outlined the idea and described the vase. Later, he sent pictures showing the exact size and color. Subodh Gupta and Wayne King worked out the formula for the glass. The shop made a wooden mould, and Hot Metal produced some samples. When Tom visited and brought the original vase just a few weeks later, he saw the samples and exclaimed 'That's our vase!'"

In total, Fenton's product development effort took most of a year, and project engineer Tom Bobbitt headed the team. The goal seemed simple enough—replicate a century-old cameo vase—but considerable time went into researching various processes that would create just the right effect. The vases were blown in paste moulds, and the work—

making 30,000 vases—kept two blow shops busy throughout the spring and summer of 1984, a time when production in some other areas had been scaled back.

An article by Bill in "The Fenton World" newsletter adds these details: "Richard Delaney worked tirelessly to develop the decorative process which so closely simulates the original cameo effect. Roger Hoover and Cecil Valentine controlled the etching process with jig design and fabrication help of Herb Fenton and Sonny Bruce. Bud Ward, Hot Metals Superintendent, guided production with the cooperation of blow shop heads Dick Maidens and Bob Hays." Richard recalls the importance of this order: "Tom Bobbitt got me out of church several times, and we went to the plant on Sunday to work on something for the vase project."

The blown vase was acid finished on the exterior to recreate the surface look of the original, and the floral motif and butterflies were replicated with special decals obtained through the Instar Supply Company. The wide white bands were handpainted, and the decorators used the pointed tip of the brush handle to remove a narrow band of paint, adding to the desired "cameo" look of the piece.

When the "Avon vase" (as it became known throughout the plant) made its debut at a press party

Don Cunningham

at the Cincinnati Art Museum, the original piece and Fenton's replica were side by side in a showcase. "I think ours was on the right," Bill remembers, "but I found myself looking down at the card to be sure!"

Another Avon project pushed Fenton to its limits during the winter of 1986. A Far East supplier was unable to fill the order, so Avon turned to Fenton for 75,000 bells to be given to sales associates on the occasion of Avon's 100th Anniversary. Fenton first suggested a custom-decorated bell from the regular line, but cost considerations led Avon to reject this choice. Finally, it was decided that machine-made wine glasses from France would be shipped to Fenton, where the foot would be taken off, followed by grinding and polishing. Pad printing with greyish silver ink to simulate etching ("AVON 100") would be done on the bowl, and a clapper would be inserted using an epoxy glue.

Striving to meet March delivery deadlines, Fenton's work began in late January when 36,000 crystal wine glasses arrived at Wood County Airport. About fifty Fenton employees were involved in various stages of the operation, which required most to wear white gloves. The clappers were glued in and allowed to dry on a pegboard rigged up by retiree Herb Fenton (there were problems with the epoxy, however, and some clappers fell out later). Fenton completed about 15,000 bells per week, but the shifting of personnel made it difficult to keep up with other scheduled production. Shortly after the last lot of bells was shipped, the company had an "all-factory buffet" to celebrate the occasion.

In the mid-1980s, Fenton hired Don Cunningham to join Pat Clark in Special Products. A Pennsylvania native, Don graduated from Otterbein College and served in the Air Force before returning to Mt. Pleasant, Pa., to work in his father's hardware business. Don was a time study

analyst at the L. E. Smith Glass Co., and he went to the Viking Glass Company in New Martinsville as plant manager in 1978. Don handled private mould accounts and became familiar with specialized machinery. He helped develop a multi-station machine to make paperweight blanks.

Unsure of Viking's future after its owners relinquished control in 1986, Don considered a plant manager's job at the Super Glass Co., in Brooklyn. They were involved with blown lighting goods, but Don didn't really want to live in the area, although he was offered the position. He also turned down a managerial job at a Michigan-based pottery.

Finally, Don spoke with Tom Fenton, whom he knew from various manufacturer's meetings. Tom conferred with George, who had recently become Fenton's president, and they invited Don for an interview. Fenton wanted to expand its private mould business, and Don was the sort of person they needed, well-versed in glassmaking and familiar with the sales side of special orders and private mould work. "Why didn't you call us sooner?," Frank asked. "I had procrastinated," Don recalled in 1995, "because I knew the hand plants were generally in a down time. I'd always regarded Fenton as the 'Cadillac' of the industry, and I always had great respect for Frank and the whole operation."

Don occupied Pat Clark's old digs near the plant's office entrance, and Pat moved next door after the telephone switching equipment was relocated. Joyce Sims was responsible for records regarding both special products and private moulds, and Trish Mahlmeister came in to handle this aspect of the sandcarving division. During the late 1980s, more and more of Fenton's special orders were funneled to Don. Frank continued to deal with collector's clubs seeking souvenirs, while Bill and Shelley worked closely with QVC.

In 1989, Joe Delisle was added to the staff to replace Pat Clark and continue the licensed and premium sandcarved segment of Fenton's business. Pat left Fenton to go to Crystal Graphics, an Akron, Ohio-based firm which did sandcarving and was interested in licensed products. Although the company acquired the rights to logos such as Coor's and did intricate sandcarvings of wildlife

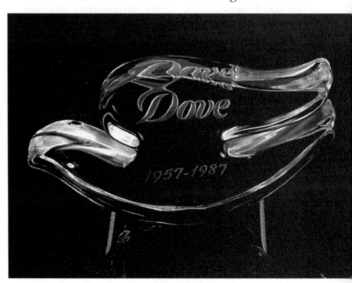

Dove paperweight.

Fenton made the sandcast pieces for this Dan Dailey creation, which was installed at the New York headquarters of The Dreyfus Fund.

scenes for Remington Arms, Crystal Graphics went out of business. Pat worked for a time in advertising specialties before retiring and returning to Marietta. "I never should have left Fenton," he said in an interview (Pat passed away in March, 1996).

Fenton made animal figurines (5151 Bear and 5163 Bird) in crystal for the Princess House party plan, a division of the Colgate Palmolive Company. This became a high-volume operation during the summer and fall of 1986, when Princess House needed more than 115,000 of these animals.

A new continuous tank for crystal glass spurred Fenton's prospects for private mould work. Don Cunningham recalls many orders for "icebergs" and other engraver's blanks intended for paperweights. In 1987, Ogilvy and Mather, a prestigious New York advertising agency, contacted Don to order 8,000 special paperweights for executive gifts. Fenton made the mould, and Don enjoyed the challenge of its technical problems. Shaped like the logo for Dove brand soap, these were sandcarved "Dove 1957-1987".

Also among Fenton's more interesting special order work was architectural glass, such as the large sandcast pieces created by artist Dan Dailey and installed in the Rainbow Room atop Rockefeller Center in New York City. Other sandcast pieces were done for the Chicago Board of Trade offices as well as Marietta Memorial Hospital. Fenton's Dennis Lumbatis co-ordinated the casting of these blocks.

Among the most important private mould accounts was Tiara Exclusives, a party plan associated with Lancaster Colony Corporation, which also owns the Indiana Glass Company. A former Fenton vice-president, Joe Ehnot, called Bill Fenton about the possibilities of Fenton making glass for Tiara. An agreement was reached wherein Fenton supplied Tiara's articles for a margin over cost. This provided steady work for Fenton employees, although it was not particularly profitable.

When Tiara wanted items made in Dusty Rose, Fenton enhanced its melting capacity by making the color in day tanks instead of smaller pots. Fenton also made other glassware for Lancaster Colony, such as large punch bowls for restaurant salad bars.

In January 1977, Fenton began its association with Candle-Land Parties of Myerstown, Pa. This organization, developed by Fred and Linda Strobel after consulting with Don Fenton and Fenton rep Tom Stork, sponsors home sales parties in the eastern Pennsylvania area. Sales were quite strong in the late 1980s, and Fenton continues to maintain a close relationship with Candle-Land in 1996.

In 1996, Don Cunningham remains involved with all phases of Fenton's private accounts—design, mould costing, production and, if necessary, sandcarving or decorating. He enjoys the challenges of this work, especially the design and mouldmaking needed for a unique piece. Don summed up his attitude this way: "We can make it! What is it?"

When Pascal, a California-based artist who had done some miniature glass sculptures, telephoned Fenton about reproducing her creations, Don thought Fenton could do the job and asked for photographs. To his surprise, she called again the very next day—from the Wood County Airport—asking him to pick her up for a visit to the factory. "She was very well-dressed and flamboyant, with long blond hair all piled up on top of her head," he said. "Everyone wondered who in the world she was when I took her on a tour of the plant." She left several glass sculpture originals, and Don worked with a sandcasting company using extraordinarily fine materials to create the moulds. One of the finished pieces, a horse's head, was used in fundraising by the athletic department at the University of Southern California.

Sandcarving

In the 1980s, it became apparent that Fenton's acid-etching division would shut down. The expense of meeting environmental regulations and other cost considerations were making the unit's viability suspect. It was phased out in early 1990, and the company discontinued making Crystal Velvet pets. Fenton had also been sandblasting ware to impart a satin finish for decorated ware. The 1980s saw a new technology, sandcarving, become established.

Sandcarving is akin to sandblasting because of the equipment used to propel the "sand" (actually powdered

aluminum oxide), but there are some key differences. The term "sandblast" is generally reserved for an all-over treatment which imparts a uniform, satin-like (but somewhat chalky) finish. Sandblasting was used instead of etching in conjunction with some Fenton colors, although etching provides a somewhat better surface for handpainted decorations.

Beginning in the late 1970s, Fenton used sandblasting equipment, including a four-station automatic machine, to create the satin finish on these colors: Lavender Satin (LN), Blue Satin (BA), White Satin (WS) and Custard Satin (CU). The pale Custard Satin was a splendid background for various handpainted decorations in the 1970s and early 1980s, and some of Fenton's most successful and long-lived motifs, such as the popular Log Cabin on Custard, may be found on this hue.

Sandcarving, which is often, but not always, done on crystal glass, first involves the application of a stencil or mask to a pre-determined area, typically one relatively smooth and free from pattern elements or mould seams. The mask protects selected areas of the surface and allows other areas to be exposed to the abrasive action of the powder. The mask must adhere very tightly to the glass so that powder does not get under it, and the mask must be durable to resist the direct bite of the aluminum oxide particles propelled by air pressure. The sandcarver must guage the proper time for exposing the glass surface to the action of the powder to achieve the desired depth and other effects.

Unlike acid etching, which renders only the very topmost surface of the glass opaque, sandcarving creates fine gradations and intricate details as well as interesting shadows and other interpretations that some feel can rival nineteenth-century cameo glass. Called "stage-blasting" or "multi-level sandcarving," this treatment involves several "pulls" of the mask. After working the initial areas as desired, the sandcarver removes parts of the mask to expose other areas. These second and third pulls enable the sandcarver to create various artistic effects. Fenton's Richard Delaney and David Rawson became deeply interested in this technique.

In the early 1980s, Richard was a member of Fenton's Design Committee, a group which met regularly to work on ideas and items for the company's regular giftware line. A West Virginia native, he had come to Fenton in 1973, shortly after graduating from Glenville State College with a major in art and a minor in English. He began as a decorator doing handpainting, and he recalls Fenton's popular Violets in the Snow among his earliest jobs.

When the decorating department expanded in the mid-1970s and a second shift was added, Richard was chosen to teach the new decorators who were learning to paint various motifs. He is now supervisor of decorating services and sandcarving; at one time he was in charge of the "whole basement" including acid etch, decorating, and pad printing as well as the glass repair area. In the late 1970s, he began to experiment with sandcarving, using a large nozzle sandblaster.

(left)

This sandcarved replica of a prize fight ticket was made for Donald Trump.

60

FENTON

Covered sandcarved
Apothecary and
Candy Jars.
Ideal for food
premiums or just
as a functional item.
Your design, logo,
or trademark
intaglio carved
in deep multi-
levels.

8076
32 oz. Apothecary
8¼"

8077
48 oz. Apothecary
10¾"

5¾" 16 oz. Apothecary
8075

8088
24 oz. Covered Candy
7"

Custom Sandcarved Products

Recognition Awards

Recognition Awards include solid walnut wood bases.
Decanters, Bowls and Plates are full lead crystal. Prices
include individual names and years of service. Camera ready
artwork is needed with initial order.

8068
Decanter with base

8065
6½" Lead Crystal Bowl
with base

8011
9" Lead Crystal Plate with base

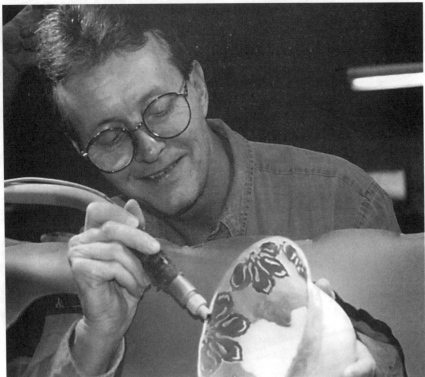

Richard Delaney

Fenton's "Shakerville."

Richard traveled to the Cleveland area with Pat Clark to go to DM Corp. to obtain various decals and to see designer Robert Michael Yates. The DM firm actually fabricated vinyl masks suitable for sandcarving, not decals, so a delighted Richard returned home with many sample masks for use in sandcarving research and trials. At Yates' sandcarving studio in Cleveland, Pat and Richard saw sandcarving equipment with small nozzles, and they learned more about sandcarving technology.

When Pat and Richard visited, Yates' employees were hard at work filling a large order for the Bradford Exchange. Later, Fenton made plates for the Bradford Exchange, using crystal from the new continuous tank. After the plates were sandcarved (to depict Orion or a similar figure), they were ground and polished using motorized tabletop surfaces to impart gentle motion. The three-step grinding and polishing operation involved a muddy mixture of water and cerium oxide, and the surroundings in Fenton's Cold Metal finishing area had to be protected from the grime by floor-to-ceiling plastic sheets. Fenton employees called the place "Shakerville."

Yates later did design work for Fenton, including sandcarved pieces for the Connoisseur Collection as well as the sandcarved crystal Statue of Liberty plate which was in the line. Yates passed away in 1993.

In March, 1981, Richard Delaney brought several sandcarved floral motifs for the Design Committee's consideration. These were done on various transparent glass colors as well as on black glass and some cased pieces. The group liked these items, and Frank Fenton commented that the sandcarving technique on cased glass might be used for some attractive limited edition items. About two years later, three sandcarved vases in "Sculptured Rose Quartz" were in the first Connoisseur Collection.

Richard Delaney's iris design was in the regular Fenton line, and it was shown in the Catalog Supplement for January, 1982. Sandcarved on amethyst glass (IY), it was one of two treatments in Fenton's "Iris Collection." The other treatment was a handpainted iris on "Bone White" glass (IN). In the Catalog Supplement, sandcarving was described as "the newest design innovation by Fenton."

Several sandcarved items appear in the May 1982, Catalog Supplement. These include a cobalt blue 7561 vase with a floral motif and 7488 temple jar with a butterfly design (both bear code KY), as well as hurricane lamps with poinsettias (PN) or love birds (LQ) and similar Astral Candlelights.

In the 1983-84 Fenton catalog, a new sandcarved motif, Love Birds on Cobalt (LK), appears. According to a letter to Fenton reps, these pieces "have added white paint to [the] carved area for extra definition." This technique for augmentation was also used in seven sandcarved items in cobalt blue which were being marketed through the West Virginia University bookstore in the spring of 1983; the sandcarved WVU emblems were enhanced with gold paint.

In 1984, Fenton issued the first sandcarved plate in what was dubbed the Liberty Commemorative Series. Designed by Yates and called "Liberty—The Gift," this plate, which retailed for $75.00, was a numbered limited edition of 19,500. The two other plates were not produced. Century Standard Crystal of Oak Brook, Illinois, contracted with Fenton to produce a plate bearing the seal of the State of Illinois.

Except for appearances in the Connoisseur Series, sandcarved pieces were generally absent from the regular Fenton line after the mid-1980s. Richard Delaney's increased knowledge of sandcarving techniques, however, had quite an influence upon the expansion of the company's Special Products department.

Chapter Twenty-Four
FENTON AND QVC

As this is being written in 1996, the QVC program has proven to be one of Fenton's very best customers. Additionally, Fenton is one of the top-selling collectibles marketed by QVC, which claimed to reach about 60 million homes in 1995. Fenton feels strongly that its exposure on QVC has attracted many new customers and collectors, those who saw Fenton glass first on the broadcasts and later sought additional items through traditional Fenton outlets.

Beginning in October, 1988, Bill Fenton, Chairman of the Board, made regular appearances on QVC with Fenton glass. In fact, Bill was QVC's first "celebrity guest," although the significance of this certainly escaped everyone involved at the time! QVC's Bob Bowersox hosted a few early shows featuring Fenton, but Steve Bryant became established as the regular host. The various QVC shows—typically one to three hours (and, occasionally, four hours)—featured a wide variety of Fenton items, ranging from relatively low-priced gifts to signed, limited edition pieces. Occasionally, Bill would be linked from home to QVC by telephone during a shorter program so that he could talk about the glass and converse with callers.

The QVC organization is an interesting story in itself. QVC was founded by Joe Segel, who had been instrumental in the success of the Franklin Mint, a marketer of collectibles whose ads appeared in Sunday newspaper supplements and other publications. In September, 1986, QVC "went public," offering two million shares of stock. The television broadcasts began in November, 1986. Sears Roebuck and QVC began a business relationship shortly thereafter, and the number of homes reached by QVC has grown rapidly, with millions being added each year. Unlike some television merchandising operations, QVC (which stands for "Quality, Value and Convenience") focuses on high quality collectibles, jewelry and other merchandise.

The Fenton company's initial contact with QVC came via Shelley Fenton's association with the Franklin Mint's Whitney Smith. In her position with Fenton's private mould and special market customers, Shelley had worked with Smith, who was employed by the Franklin Mint from 1980 to 1986 in the area of product development.

After Smith left the Franklin Mint, she became a freelance consultant. Through an affiliation with QVC, she was part of an ongoing effort to seek collectibles for QVC programs. Because of the success in Franklin Mint programs, Capodimonte porcelain was being sold on QVC. Naturally, Smith also thought of Fenton, and she spoke with Shelley about possible Fenton items for inclusion on the program. An important consideration was the fact that Fenton products are American-made.

QVC's Executive Vice-President (later President) Doug Briggs and Whitney Smith visited Fenton, and Bill and Shelley later journeyed to West Chester, Pa. with samples of glassware. Their discussions centered upon possible Fenton products for sale through QVC, and they decided to offer the popular 5151 Birthstone Bear. QVC ordered 100 of each of the twelve months

of the year, and these were shipped February 12, 1988.

Fenton was well aware of the great potential in this initial order. Notes on internal Fenton documents stressed the importance of concerted attention to high quality standards and concluded that "a lot is riding on this." In retrospect, that may be a bit of an understatement, for the Birthstone Bears just "flew out the door" during the broadcast. They were sold at the regular retail price plus a shipping/handling charge.

QVC soon ordered more and more Fenton products. A few items, especially during 1988, were drawn from Fenton's regular line, but everyone soon agreed that the collectible items worked best when they were made exclusively for QVC. Fenton's capacity to make collectible glass and to develop new colors and interesting treatments was essential to the growing relationship. Many QVC items reflect Fenton's glassmaking knowledge and skills in both Hot Metal and Cold Metal: gold, ruby and other colors which must be warmed in to strike; overlays; crests; handles on baskets; various crimps; original decorative motifs; and painting/frit combinations.

During 1988-1990, Fenton produced a wide range of items for QVC. These included items from the regular Fenton line, beyond the 5151 Birthstone Bear such as offerings from the Pearly Sentiments (PT) group. Sometimes, QVC offered Fenton limited edition pieces (such as Mother's Day bells or Christmas bells) which were also available through regular Fenton outlets. In these cases, QVC typically ordered several hundred bells from a limited edition of 2500.

Most of the Fenton glassware offered via QVC was made exclusively for this market. Selected items were numbered, limited editions, such as the 7562 VQ 1989 Valentine's Day bell (350), but most were Fenton shapes made in special colors or with treatments not found in the regular line.

Fenton made some special signed pieces for QVC, too. In 1989, Bill Fenton's signature was handpainted on the bottom of the 7532 QX Rosalene 9" basket, which had been decorated with handpainted pink roses. In 1990, a diamond-point stylus was used for Bill's signa-

Bill Fenton and QVC host Steve Bryant describe Fenton glass during a broadcast in 1990.

ture on the 9134 DN Butterfly and Berry basket (this piece is iridized Dusty Rose with a milk glass crest and handle). Later, Fenton used a decal process for the various Fenton family signature pieces sold through QVC.

Among the most popular Fenton items sold through QVC between 1988-1990 were these: 5165 cat in Shell Pink with various floral decorations, the 8335 XB open edge basket and the 8428 XB Butterfly and Berry bowl (both in Black Carnival glass), the 9560 GZ Templebells bell in Holiday Green Carnival glass and Blue Opalescent (BX) items made in 1990. Some of the Christmas and Mother's Day bells sold quite well, as did the Easter bell for 1990. These and many other Fenton items for QVC are shown in color in this book.

Although Fenton was pleased at the results of the QVC broadcasts and the prospects for increased sales, the reactions of established Fenton reps and dealer accounts needed to be addressed. Understandably, some of them might feel that Fenton glass on QVC would cut into their potential sales.

Although most Fenton items sold through QVC were not otherwise available, some were articles from the regular line. In a letter to Fenton reps (dated October 4, 1989), Bill assured them that regular line items sold through QVC would sell at the full regular retail prices plus appropriate charges for shipping and handling. The letter continued as follows: "We did not want to do anything that would disturb our regular retail accounts and felt that this would be a great advertising medium for Fenton and for these products. This is the way it has worked out...It is our feeling that this gets the Fenton name in front of many millions of prospective cus-tomers. It is probably the best advertising campaign that we could have to help your dealers sell our products and to protect them in their pricing at the same time."

In a subsequent letter (August 1, 1990) to Fenton reps, Bill called attention to a show scheduled to air August 4, 1990, on QVC: "It does reach many people and it is helping to build a recognition of the Fenton name and the fact that we are handmade in America. It is advertising that we could not afford to buy, but I believe it does help you tremendously by creating a greater demand for Fenton products and a recognition of our name." Bill also noted that exposure on QVC had been at least partially responsible for the strong sales of Fenton's Birthstone Bears over the past two years.

A vital element in Fenton's success with QVC was the company's ability to meet QVC's deadlines, quality standards and stringent shipping and packaging requirements. Fenton products must arrive at QVC's West Chester, Pa. facility on schedule, and the proper cartons must be ready for QVC's shipping procedures. QVC does not unwrap the merchandise except to check quality, so Fenton is responsible for packaging. A tight deadline and a large quantity can strain Fenton's personnel, but the company has been able to meet its obligations to QVC without affecting its service to regular customers. One Fenton employee remarked that "it's always an effort, but we know it's worth it."

Reflecting upon the company's association with QVC, Bill Fenton noted that "a very strong bond of both business and personal relationships has developed. Lasting friendships and mutual respect between Fenton and QVC employees has built a sound future together."

Chapter Twenty-Five
THE COLLECTORS
by Ferill J. Rice

For many of you, this book is your first encounter with Fenton. Let me introduce the Fenton Art Glass Collectors of America, Inc. The organization was founded as a not-for-profit international collectors club in Appleton, Wisconsin, on January 4, 1976. The founders incorporated for the purpose of studying and preserving American-made glass, with a special emphasis on the Fenton Art Glass Company.

In 1996, the organization has approximately 5,500 members enjoying the fellowship that is such a positive pleasure of belonging to the group. On January 1, 1996, membership number 13,485 was issued (once you obtain a membership number, that number is yours forever and is never reissued).

When I was asked to do this chapter, I thought it would be easy, but the longer I worked, the more difficult it became. How do I write a history of our organization? In writing this account of the Fenton Art Glass Collectors of America, Inc. for the 1980s, I must mention names and events, for our history is the story of people.

In April 1977, the Fenton Finders of Wisconsin (our original name) started letting it be known that anyone could join for a fee of $4.00 for the first member in a household, and one additional dollar for other members in the same household. Membership quickly grew, and by August, when the first convention was held, we had 57 members (and $111.01 in the bank!).

The first convention at the Valley Inn in Neenah, Wisconsin, featured a display of Fenton glass. Members brought glass, and we lined the walls of a banquet room with glassware beautifully displayed on colorful tablecloths. We publicized the event as "free to the public" over radio and television, and over 1000 people visited in one afternoon. We even had a door prize! We gained new members, and everyone felt our first convention was a huge success.

Four of our newest members—Lois and Bob Ratcliff of Romney, Indiana, and Hermena and Ralph Garrettson of Anderson, Indiana—traveled to be with us. The first officers and board were elected, and Lois Ratcliff and Ralph Garrettson were elected to the board along with Bob Cowan. The original ten members of the Fenton Finders of Wisconsin had been acting as the board. Officers elected for one year terms were: President, Otis L. Rice; First Vice President, Donald L. Moore; Second Vice President, Arvin T. Wolfgram; Recording Secretary, Betty J. Wolfgram; Corresponding Secretary, Ferill J. Rice; Treasurer, Lois Rehmer; and Historian, Sylvia Landry.

At a special meeting in July, 1977, the club voted to grant Otis L. Rice permission to get a loan to finance the cost of having butterfly paperweights made. As it turned out, we had the ruby carnival Butterfly covered candy box for our first souvenir instead. This was a difficult piece of glass for Fenton to make; the ruby turned amberina, and the square corners often broke. We ended up with many more lids than bottoms. We quickly sold all pieces made, however, so the venture was a success.

Prior to the 1977 convention, we discussed naming the newsletter, and each member was to bring ideas to the meeting. Betty Wolfgram had discovered that a preva-

lent theme in Fenton glass patterns was a butterfly. We added "Net," since all good collectors use this to catch butterflies. Later, William Heacock named a rare Fenton glass pattern Butterfly Net in honor of the Fenton Art Glass Collectors newsletter. This pattern is now a registered trademark of the FAGCA.

We decided our next convention should be near Williamstown so that we could visit the Fenton factory. The convention was held at the Holiday Inn in Parkersburg in August, 1978. In 1979, we went to the Lafayette Hotel in Marietta, holding our convention there until 1989, when we returned to the Holiday Inn in Parkersburg.

The 1980 Convention theme was "Diamonds" to recognize the 75th Anniversary of the Fenton Art Glass Co. The theme for the displays was "Jewels," and the winning table (a display of Emerald Crest) was presented by the Fenton Finders of Michigan. Over the years, the basic rules for this important convention event have remained the same. Families and individuals may set up one table in the display room using the theme for the year. Children are encouraged to participate and have done so since the second convention, with their own awards being given. In 1980, over 400 registered for the convention. The souvenir chairman was Helen Warner, and the souvenir was a Velva Rose Butterfly on a stand. We finally had our butterfly!

Along with Bill Fenton, FAGCA members Ferill Rice, Joan Illk and Charles Illk check on the progress of glass being made for the club.

Officers for 1980-81 were: President, Otis Rice; first Vice President, Stanton G. Darling; second Vice President, Helen Warner; Editor and Secretary, Ferill J. Rice; Treasurer, Glenn Huguet; and Historian, Sylvia Landry. Thanks to Stanton Darling, we received provisional 501(c)(3) tax exempt status from the Internal Revenue Service (we were granted full status in September, 1981).

We spread the word about the club and the fun of collecting Fenton glass. Members spoke to other groups: Roserita Ziegler at Wheaton Village in New Jersey and the Encore Convention in Kansas; Kitty and Russell Umbraco at the Marine Depression Glass Club; Ferill Rice at the Fenton Finders of Michigan; and Bill Heacock at the Michigan Depression Glass Club. In 1985, Bill Heacock visited the Heavenly Production show in San Jose, California, and also spoke at the Fenton Finders of Northern California meeting. Members have always been generous with their expertise, and many are quite knowledgeable in areas of glassmaking, history, and other things you might want to know about the glass industry in the United States.

Over 350 people crowded into the Sternwheel Room at the Lafayette Hotel for our 1980 banquet. Our first banquet speaker in 1978 had been Dr. Robert P. Fischer, Director of Personnel Research at Fenton, and in 1979, it was Chairman of the Board Frank M. Fenton. In 1980, it was Bill Fenton, president of the Fenton Art Glass Co. He told us about many things that had happened since his joining the family business. These three speakers enlightened us about the glass Fenton had made in the past, and they spiced their talks with humorous happenings at the factory and acquainted us with various workers.

The Convention theme for 1981 was Song Titles. After the display tables are set up during each convention, Frank M. Fenton tours the room to determine if all pieces of glass on these tables are indeed Fenton. For several years, Bill Heacock assisted Frank and Helen Warner, who was Frank Fenton's secretary for many years.

Over the years many humorous and educational things have come out of this event. One year, the Fenton Finders of Wisconsin deliberately put a very badly damaged Imperial cup on our table. We had clued Frank Fenton in and had placed a hidden bucket containing rocks behind the table. Frank was to spy the cup and, with an appropriate remark ("how did a piece of Imperial glass get into this room?"), throw the cup into the bucket, breaking it to emphasize the question.

In 1981, the FAGCA sponsored an antique show held on the Marietta College campus with Kay Darling as manager and members of the Fenton Finders of the Mid-Ohio Valley helping. It was a very successful show.

The 1981 Convention was also special in that we had two sets of "honeymooners" with us. Marve and Sandra Rose of Green Bay, Wisconsin, were married two weeks prior to the convention, and they spent their stay in the honeymoon suite of the Lafayette Hotel. The other couple—Dick and Mary Koebbe of Loveland, Ohio—were married on the Saturday prior to the convention. In 1982 the honeymooners attending the Convention were Kay and Gerry Wahl of Green Bay, Wisconsin. August 1986 saw us with another honeymoon couple. Van Funderburk of Land O' Lakes, Florida, and his beautiful bride were married just one week when they came to the convention.

Charters were given to six new clubs in 1981: Fenton Finders of the Mid-Ohio Valley; Fenton Finders of the Toledo, Ohio area; Fenton Finders of Greater Kansas City; Fenton Finders of Wyoming, Chapter one; Fenton Finders of Wyoming, Chapter Two; and the Fenton Finders of the Mile High City. There were requests for people to help form local chapters—some of which succeeded while others did not. What the secret is to the formation of a successful organization such as ours, I am not sure. It takes a great amount of work and dedication. Long hours and enthusiasm are necessary, too.

At an IRS audit in 1981, we came through with flying colors, but one of the important items stressed was that we needed to develop a greater educational program. Because of this, the board gave Ferill Rice another job, that of educational chairperson with Helen Warner as her assistant. This is the position by which our entire club retains its IRS status and its place in today's collectors world. The auditor recommended that the club become more involved in public displays of old glass and stressed the word "old."

The Fenton Finders of Wisconsin have worked diligently on this. A display at the Holiday Inn in Green Bay had over 750 pieces of glass for a one-day event that drew over 500 people, as did a display at the gym in Seymour, Wisconsin. Others were held at the Neville Public Museum in Green Bay and the Paper Valley Hotel in Appleton as well as many banks and libraries. Most recently, there were two events at the Bergstrom-Mahler Paperweight Museum in Neenah. Once, the FAGCA even had a display at a local jail.

The display at the Neville Public Museum in Green Bay was there for two months with several evening lectures presented by members of the Fenton Finders of Wisconsin. Many people throughout the Fox Valley became acquainted with the history of the glass industry. We ended the exhibit with a two day extravaganza. Frank Fenton came to Wisconsin to join us at the museum to celebrate the exhibit, which had been seen by over 40,000. More people visited this exhibit than any previous two months in the museum's history.

In June, 1982, we hired a second part-time employee, Suzanne Bunkert. The work had become too much for Betty Wolfgram, who had been working part-time, and for Ferill Rice who was a full-time volunteer. Both Betty and Sue averaged 20 hours each per week.

Many new things came from the Capital Expenditure Committee in 1982. During the 1982 convention, it was decided that we should establish a scholarship fund. Two $1000 scholarships were offered in 1983. Mary Clapper of Minerva, Ohio, was chairman of this project with Stan Darling on the committee. In August 1983, scholarships were presented to Kevin Gooder and Faye Osborn. A year later, the board discontinued the scholarships to use our monies for the office, since our expenses were increasing ten-fold.

In 1983, the board determined we had enough funds and knowledge to print what was to become known as the "catalog reprints." Helen Warner, Paul Klosterman, Ed Tell and Ferill Rice were appointed to the committee. These reprints covered the years of 1953 to 1966, and we eventually added what we had of the 1949 Fenton price list. This was a three-ring binder with selected pages from the catalogs of those years that had not been reprinted in the three Fenton books published by Antique Publications.

The 1982 banquet speaker was Bill Heacock, followed in 1983 by Dr. Eugene Murdock, author of the Fenton history. In 1982, Mrs. Jacqueline Proctor of Makakilo, Hawaii, attended the convention. We had members in all 50 states, and by 1989, we had members in the United Kingdom, New Zealand, Australia and Canada.

Until June, 1984, the FAGCA home office was in Appleton, Wisconsin. At that time, we moved to Williamstown, and have been there ever since. At first,

THE FENTON ART GLASS COLLECTORS OF AMERICA, INC.

1980 Souvenir

The Year of the Butterfly in Velva Rose. First introduced in the twenties, this sparkling satin iridescent glass treatment is being brought back this year to help commemorate Fenton's 75th Anniversary.

FAGCA provides the Fenton collector this "one-time only" opportunity to acquire this beautiful Velva Rose Butterfly on a stand. Each piece bears the FAGCA butterfly and date.

Sales limited to two butterflies for each membership card in a family.

Orders will not be accepted after August 1, 1980.

Please use the order blank enclosed.

we could not find a suitable office, so the Fenton company rented us quarters among the offices at the factory. In the fall of 1990, we moved to East Fifth St. and started a search for something larger. In 1993, our present home was found at 702 West Fifth Street.

In 1987, Chari Sherrill came to work for the FAGCA. What a lucky day it was for us. She has been with us through good times and bad, and a more dedicated employee an organization such as ours could never find.

Over the years, the FAGCA has had only six Presidents, including the present one. Otis Rice served from 1977-84 and Bill Ehrsam from 1984 to 1988, Kay Wahl served from 1988-91, and David Nielsen from 1991 to 1993. Ferill Rice served from 1993 to 1995, and the current President is Arthur Gilbert.

The annual convention is the highlight of any year. Not only are there special factory tours, but we also have seminars to learn about glass making, glass collecting, old and new types of glass, and the Fenton organization. Some interesting seminars have been presented, such as one done by Frank Fenton on the Barber Collection and glass artist Robert Barber. Howard Seufer, a longtime Fenton employee now retired, has done several seminars, but one that stood out was his discussion of moulds. We have also had seminars on the decorating of Fenton glass by Fenton decorators. Collectors can learn a great deal by attending conventions.

At a convention in the mid-1980s, FAGCA members brought glass for photography as Bill Heacock and Frank Fenton were working on the third Fenton book, which covers the 1955-1980 period. Bill passed away in 1988 before the project was complete, but Jim Measell and Frank Fenton finished the book and it was published in 1989.

The collectors who belong to the Fenton Art Glass Collectors of America, Inc. have a chance to obtain Fenton glass made exclusively for the club. Every year since that first ruby iridized butterfly box, we have had a souvenir made. During the factory tours for the convention attendees, a special glass is made that can be purchased by those members at the convention. Over the years, the club has had other glass made to finance various activities.

The club also owns two moulds. Our mug has a butterfly caught in a net. More recently, a Happy Cat mould was made. This is a small (4 1/2" tall) cat similar to the Fenton 5177 Alley Cat. The FAGCA moulds have been produced in several of Fenton's most interesting and collectible glass colors.

The growth of Fenton glass collectors and the FAGCA contributed to the success of the Fenton Art Glass Company during the 1980s. While the club was not established for this purpose, collectors' inclinations turned more and more to glass being made and decorated at present. Many collectors are not aware of the great joy of searching for a particular older piece and finally finding it. Instead, collectors seem to be turning to the task of finding every piece known to be made in a certain color, type, or decoration. In the past, glass companies made glass to market as gifts and for the housewife to use. Now the companies are thinking more and more about the collector.

The following national organizations have been formed by Fenton collectors and are dedicated to learning more about Fenton glass. Each club offers its own newsletters about Fenton glass, and each holds a national convention. Some have local chapters across the country. These organizations are completely independent from the Fenton Art Glass Company. The glass company supplies information and other non-monetary support. The organizations are good sources of information as well as a great way to meet people with similar interests.

Fenton Art Glass Collectors of America, Inc. (FAGCA)
P. O. Box 384
Williamstown, WV 26187

National Fenton Glass Society (NFGS)
P. O. Box 4008
Marietta, OH 45750

Pacific Northwest Fenton Association (PNFA)
8225 Kilchis River Rd.
Tillamook, OR 97141

During the 1980s, Fenton made small quantities of antique-style glass for a variety of retail dealers. These items do not appear in regular Fenton catalogues or supplements, but the glass was typically made in Fenton-owned moulds. To reduce set-up costs and allow for short runs, a single mould was often used to make pieces which could be finished into a variety of shapes.

The colors and/or treatments were hues, special shapes or decorations not in the Fenton line at the time when the items were made (although they may have been in the line earlier and/or put in later!). Many colors, such as Aqua Opalescent Carnival, were quite popular with collectors who liked Victorian or early twentieth century styles.

Fenton's strongest relationship in the 1980s was probably with the Illinois-based Levay firm, but there were others—such as Doris Lechler, Dorothy Taylor and Mary Walrath—whose glassware is of interest to collectors today. For much of the 1980s, these assortments were marketed with color illustrated sheets using the phrase "for the Antique Trade." Although these pieces carried the Fenton logo, the company was not comfortable with the phrase, so it was dropped and "Collector's Extravaganza" began in 1988. In the 1990s, these offerings were designated as Fenton's "Historic Collection."

Glass for Levay

The Levay Distributing Company was located at 209 East Vandalia Street in Edwardsville, Illinois. The organization was run by Gary Levi, and its name comes from the surname of his paternal grandfather, Michael John Levay. Although the firm maintained a retail store and a showroom, much of its business was done by mail order. Dorothy Taylor's *Encore by Dorothy, Book I* (1979) and *Encore by Dorothy, Book II* (1979) are good sources on the glass made for Levay by various companies in the 1970s.

Levay offered "assortments" of antique-style glass in colors that were not part of the regular Fenton line. Sometimes, orders were processed by Levay and forwarded to the Fenton plant in Williamstown, but, on most occasions, the glassware was shipped to the Levay showroom in Edwardsville. The articles which made up the early Levay assortments in the 1980s were determined after production at Fenton so that sufficient inventory would be available to fill anticipated orders.

Levay was very interested in making old patterns—such as Fenton's Butterfly and Berry, Greentown's Cactus, Hobbs-Brockunier's Hobnail, or Northwood's Grape and Cable—in antique-style colors, particularly opalescent effects or Carnival hues such as aqua opalescent or red. Many of the articles produced by Fenton for Levay were functional pieces (bowls, butterdishes, creamer/sugar sets, punch sets, and water sets), but others were decorative to the point of being whimseys. These pieces all had the Fenton logo.

During 1980, Fenton produced several Carnival glass assortments for Levay. The Electric Blue Carnival Art Glass (BN) group consisted of 14 different items and was advertised as "a new color and iridescent treatment."

It was available through May 31, 1980. At this same time, Fenton also made a Poppy Gone with the Wind Lamp (limited to 500) and a Diamond Lattice 7-piece water set (limited to 300 sets) in Electric Blue Carnival.

Levay's Electric Blue Carnival (BN)

Number	Item
1707	water set
1768	cruet/stopper
5174	rabbit
5177	Alley Cat
5178	owl
8223	Orange Tree rose bowl
8295	toothpick holder
8419	Butterfly & Berry plate
8428	Butterfly & Berry bowl
9101	lamp
9123	Persian Medallion rose bowl
9133	Strawberry toothpick basket
9134	Butterfly & Berry basket
9135	Persian Medallion basket
9495	Butterfly & Berry hat

Made in 1980, these have the Fenton logo.

The Aqua Opal Carnival Glass (IO; made by iridizing Fenton's BO, blue opalescent with a marigold spray) was a selection of just five pieces (9425 ribbon candy edge 8" bowl; 9435 ribbon candy edge 8½" basket; 9436 8½" rose bowl basket; 9454 5" rose bowl; and 9456 12" swung vase), all of which were made from the "curtain pattern 1366 mould." Fenton records also indicate that the 3860 Hobnail bowl (3938) and pitcher (3764) set was being made for Levay in IQ (Blue Opalescent iridized with a light mother-of-pearl spray) about May 1, 1980, and the 3908 7-piece water set was probably made about the same time.

Several articles were added to Levay's Aqua Opalescent selection in June, 1980. The 3407 Cactus 7-piece water set consisted of a pitcher (made from the 3467 cracker jar mould) and six 3445 goblets (these were made as a limited edition of 400 sets). The 2805 Wild Rose and Bowknot student lamp was being made at this time, also as a limited edition.

There was also a Levay offering consisting of Vaseline Opalescent Hobnail (TO) articles and eight pieces of Celestial Blue Satin (ES) in the Wild Rose and Bowknot pattern. Among the Vaseline Opalescent articles was a limited edition punch set consisting of a pie crust crimped punch bowl with stand and a dozen cups. The Celestial Blue Satin was actually an acid-etched version of Fenton's standard Blue Opalescent (BO) glass. The color illustrated sheet described Celestial Blue Satin as follows: "the gentle interlacing of pure white and azure has the look of a summer sky. The satin finish gives each piece the feel of luxurious silk."

Levay's Vaseline Opalescent (TO) Hobnail

3712 . . . . .14-piece punch set (ltd. 150)
3606 . . . . .covered sugar and creamer set
3677 . . . . .covered butter
3701 . . . . .10" triple jack in the pulpit epergne
3720 . . . . .12" pie crust crimped banana stand
3795 . . . . .toothpick
3830 . . . . .10" pie crust crimped basket
3837 . . . . .7" basket
3854 . . . . .4¹/₂" ruffled top rose bowl
3861 . . . . .4¹/₄" crimped rose bowl
3869 . . . . .cruet
3924 . . . . .9" double crimped fruit bowl
3974 . . . . .4" candle holder
3995 . . . . .kitten slipper

Made in 1980, these have the Fenton logo.

Levay's Celestial Blue Satin (ES), Wild Rose and Bowknot

2823 . . . . .9" double crimped bowl
2824 . . . . .jack in the pulpit bowl
2834 . . . . .7" double crimped basket
2836 . . . . .pie crust crimped basket with
                              looped handle
2853 . . . . .5" crimped rose bowl
2854 . . . . .9" ruffled jack in the pulpit vase
2857 . . . . .7½" double crimped vase
2864 . . . . .ruffled top pitcher

Made in 1980, these have the Fenton logo.

Levay's Red Sunset Carnival (RN) Fine Cut and Grapes

9037 . . . .looped handled dbl. crimped basket
9043 . . . . .spittoon
9044 . . . . .rose bowl cupped
9046 . . . . .double crimped bowl 5½" d.
9053 . . . . .jack in the pulpit 6½" d.
9060 . . . . .6" handkerchief vase

Made in 1981, these have the Fenton logo.

In early 1981, Levay marketed a limited edition of Fenton's Butterfly and Berry pattern in Aqua Opalescent Carnival glass. These were described as the "rarest, most sought-after color of old carnival" and "signed, dated and sequentially numbered" in Levay's promotional materials. The pieces, all bearing the Fenton logo, were made in December, 1980, and the billing to Levay was handled as a "flat charge for eight hours of whimsies." There were eleven articles, all of which were available in very small quantities as noted: 8240/1 3³/₄" six-double crimped vase, iridescent inside and outside (86 made); 8240/1 3³/₄" six-double crimped vase, iridescent outside only (18 made); 8240/2 7¹/₂" looped handle six-double crimped basket, iridescent inside and outside (96 made); 8240/2 7¹/₂" looped handle six-double crimped basket, iridescent outside only (29 made); 8240/3 9" beaded top swung vase iridescent inside and outside (41 made); 8240/4 4" flared top spittoon iridescent inside and outside only (61 made); 8240/4 4" flared top spittoon iridescent outside only (7 made); 8240/5 7¹/₂" pie crust crimp oval basket iridescent inside and outside (65 made); 8240/5 7¹/₂" pie crust crimp oval basket iridescent outside only (3 made); 8240/6 3³/₄" pie crust crimp vase iridescent inside and outside (40 made); and 5¹/₂" handkerchief vase iridescent inside and outside (42 made).

An early 1981 Levay offering contained several Hobnail items in Vaseline Opalescent (TO; this was also Fenton's designation for Topaz Opalescent), as follows: 2424 4" rose bowl; 2437 7" basket; 2473 cruet; and 3908 7-piece water set.

Also in early 1981, Levay offered two more limited editions. One of these, in Red Sunset Carnival (RN [note: RN was also used for Dorothy Taylor's Red Bermuda Carnival]), consisted of six pieces, all made from the 8457 three-toed vase mould. Fenton made 1000 of each article for Levay. The pattern, called "Fine Cut and Grapes" in Levay's promotional materials, is reminiscent of Northwood's Fine Cut and Roses. The second limited edition was a 7-piece water set in Raven Carnival (XB), utilizing pitcher and tumbler moulds from Fenton's Lincoln Inn line, a popular pattern from the late 1920s.

In the spring/summer of 1981, Levay introduced 15 pieces in Purple Slag (PS) as well as ten items in Purple Stretch (VY). At the time, "slag" colors were popular in the collectibles marketplace, and Fenton's stretch-effect Velva Rose had sold well. Fenton records indicate that the purple slag glass was a combination of "mottled opal/MI and amethyst/AY."

In May-June, 1981, Levay had Fenton make several Aqua Opalescent Carnival (IO) whimsies using the 9188 Grape and Cable tobacco jar mould; these included a spittoon, a swung vase, a double crimped bowl, a banana bowl, and two baskets, including one with a looped handle. A similar order, placed in August, 1981, called for Fenton to make these pieces "in KL [a light blue called Forget-Me-Not blue] glass with transparent (light CN) dope." A Levay flyer from April, 1982, contains these color names: "Fenton Purple Carnival" and "Fenton Wistblueria."

In November, 1981, Levay had Fenton make Aqua Opalescent Carnival baskets from the 8223 Leaf and Orange Tree bowl; these have looped handles, and one basket is crimped. About the same time, four Aqua Opal Carnival items were made in the Cherry Chain motif with Orange Tree exterior. These include the following: banana bowl; bowl with ribbon candy crimped edge; 11" flat chop plate; banana basket with looped handle; fine crimped basket with looped handle; and 12-point crimped basket with looped handle. Two other Aqua Opal Carnival items were also made—Butterfly and Berry double crimped vase and Inverted Strawberry 6¹/₂" stemmed rosebowl.

Levay's Purple Slag (PS)

3667	5½" hobnail bell
3995	Kitten Slipper
5162	Rabbit
5177	Alley Cat door stop
5197	Happiness Bird
8223	Leaf and Orange Tree rose bowl
8230	Butterfly bon bon
8231	Multi-Fruit comport
8233	Orange Tree and Cherry bowl
8237	Heart & Vine bowl
8257	8" Peacock vase
8295	Strawberry toothpick holder
9133	6½" Strawberry mini-basket
9136	Orange Tree and Cherry basket [made from 8233 bowl];
9188	Grape & Cable tobacco jar

Made in 1981, these have the Fenton logo.

Levay's Purple Stretch (VY)

7505	5-piece star crimped epergne (ltd. 1000)
7509	7-piece tankard water set (ltd. 500)
5153	4" miniature Vase in Hand
7551	6" Dolphin fan vase
7563	6½" star crimped bell
7567	4" miniature basket
7581	5½" Dolphin loving cup
7590	2" toothpick holder
8435	9" Diamond & Thread pie crust crimped basket
8455	Diamond & Thread double crimped vase

Made in 1981, these have the Fenton logo.

Levay's Blue Opalescent Hobnail (BO)
Levay's Aqua Opal Carnival (IO)

3611	10-piece champagne punch set
3645	bell
3677	covered butter (not made in IO)
3701	triple jack in the pulpit epergne
3720	12" pie crust crimped banana stand
3795	toothpick holder
3834	6½" basket
3863	cruet w/stopper
3869	mini cruet w/stopper
3908	7-piece water set.

Made in 1982, these have the Fenton logo.

Levay's Red Sunset Carnival (RN)
Cactus

3407	7-piece water set
3408	covered sugar/creamer set
3426	ladies' cuspidor
3427	gentlemen's cuspidor
3429	footed double crimped compote
3431	10" double crimped basket
3432	single crimped pie crust banana basket with ribbed looped handle
3433	10" double crimped basket
3434	10" basket vase
3436	7½" double crimped basket with ribbed looped handle
3441	double crimped jack in pulpit vase
3463	cruet
3480	covered cracker jar
3483	9" swung vase
3495	toothpick holder

Made in 1982, these have the Fenton logo.

The year 1982 was among Levay's most active with Fenton products. Early in the year, a 14-piece Blue Opalescent Hobnail punch set (3712 BO consisting of punch bowl, stand and a dozen cups) was marketed, along with these articles in Red Satin (RA) Hobnail: 3608 fairy light; 3628 footed comport; 3667 bell; 3837 7" basket; 3924 9" bowl; and 3947 candleholders. A Red Satin 24" "Poppy" lamp (9101) was also being made at this time. The RA was an acid-etched version of Fenton's RU glass.

Within a few weeks, Levay added more items in Blue Opalescent Hobnail to its offerings; except for the 3677 covered butter, all of these Hobnail pieces were also available in Aqua Opal Carnival, and they were depicted together on an illustrated color sheet.

Fenton moulds were also used to produce an assortment of Red Sunset Carnival (RN) Cactus articles in March-April, 1982. The assortment included the 3407 7-piece water set, which consisted of a handled pitcher fashioned from the cracker jar base plus six goblets.

During the spring-summer of 1982, Fenton also produced Chocolate glass (CK) for Levay. In May, a few Chocolate items (8223 Leaf and Orange Tree rose bowl; 8428 Butterfly and Berry bowl; and, possibly, 9463 Nativity bell) were made as turn work. Later, there was a nice Chocolate glass assortment illustrated with a color sheet. Not illustrated (but listed in Fenton records) were two other Chocolate items for Levay—3463 Cactus cruet w/stopper and 9101 Gone with the Wind lamp. Fenton had made Chocolate glass earlier as one of its Bicentennial colors in 1976.

In May 1982, Fenton made one turn of the 9188 Grape and Cable tobacco jar for Levay, using French Opalescent glass. These were to be "made into a spittoon with top flared similar to the 3426 RN Cactus piece." Hobnail items in Cranberry Opalescent (CR) were also offered by Levay in May, 1982. There was a water set (3909, consisting of 3360 pitcher made from the 3752 11" vase and six 3947 tumblers), as well as these items: 3347 8" looped handle basket; 3362 6½" jack in the pulpit

These Chocolate glass items were made in 1982, and all have the Fenton logo except for some of the Cactus cracker jar lids.

3480 CK
Cactus Covered Cracker Jar

8402 CK
Cherries Cream
and Sugar

9003 CK
7 pc. Lincoln Inn Water Set
4½" Tumblers, 7½" Pitcher

9580 CK
Button and Arch Covered Butter

8427 CK
Oval Pinwheel
Comport

8295 CK
Strawberry Toothpick Holder

3995 CK
6" Kitten Slipper

9640 CK
Craftsman Stein

3323 PO
4½" Crimped Vase

3645 PO
Crimped Bell

3734 PO
12" Double Crimped
Basket

3306 PO
7 pc. Water Set

3303 PO
Pitcher and Bowl Set

3733 PO
Heart Relish

Deep Plum Opalescent Hobnail (1984); all pieces have the Fenton logo.

3664 PO
70 oz. Ice Lip Pitcher

3720 PO
12" Pie Crust
Crimped Banana Stand

3804 PO
3 pc. Fairy Light

3938 PO
12" Double Crimped
Hobnail Bowl

3735 PO
5½" Double Crimped Basket

Deep Plum Opalescent Hobnail (1984); all pieces have the Fenton logo.

vase; 3830 10" pie crust edge basket; 3333 8" basket; 3863 cruet with opalescent ribbed handle and French opalescent stopper; and 9201 banquet lamp.

In June 1982, Fenton made one turn of Burmese glass for Levay. Half of the items were to be made as baskets, and the other half as bowls. Some were to be satin finished by sandblasting and handpainted later. Cranberry Opalescent (CR) Coin Dot was also offered by Levay in late 1982.

In February, 1983, Levay offered Vaseline Opalescent (TO) Hobnail once again, and a small assortment of Deep Plum Opalescent Hobnail (PO) was made in May, 1984 (this color was previously made at Fenton in 1959-62). A Levay ad in the May, 1984, issue of *Glass Review* showed the 10" triple jack in the pulpit epergne and mentioned "water set, baskets, fairy lite and others." Plum Opalescent sold well, and these pieces are of interest to collectors today.

Later in 1984, Fenton made a small quantity of iridized Plum Opalescent (IP) articles for Levay. These include some of the shapes made earlier in Aqua Opal Carnival: 9425 ribbon candy edge 8" bowl; 9435 ribbon candy edge 8½" basket; 9436 8½" rose bowl basket; 8454 5" rose bowl; and 9456 12" swung vase.

These seem to be the final Levay groups made by Fenton, although Levay advertised a limited edition of 250 Alley Cat door stops in Rose Pink Carnival (probably Dusty Rose glass with an iridescent finish) in the February, 1985, issue of *Glass Review*.

Levay's Vaseline Opalescent (TO) Hobnail

3306	7-piece water set
3323	4½" cupped rose bowl
3324	9" single crimped bowl
3325	11" footed double crimped bowl
3335	double crimped basket
3337	7" double crimped basket
3392	toothpick holder
3609	salt and pepper set
3801	4-piece epergne set
3874	cornucopia candleholder
3901	cream and sugar set.

Made in 1983, these have the Fenton logo.

3701 PO
Triple Jack in the Pulpit Epergne

3638 PO
8½" Double Crimped Basket

**Deep Plum Opalescent Hobnail (1984);
all pieces have the Fenton logo.**

Levay's Cranberry Opalescent (CR) Coin Dot

1403	3-piece fairy light
1436	double crimped rose bowl
1439	small basket with candy stripe handle
1446	7" basket with candy stripe handle
1479	double crimped vase
1483	bottle vase
1489	7" jack in the pulpit vase
1493	ewer with candy stripe handle

Made in 1982, these have the Fenton logo.

The Levay firm continued its business for several years, and Gary Levi later became associated with the Westmoreland Glass Company. The Levay Distributing Company was eventually closed, but Gary Levi remained active in the glass industry as owner of the Intaglio Crystal Art Glass Company in Alton, Illinois (see *Antique Trader Weekly*, September 20, 1995). The Levis and the Fentons remain good friends and see each other often at gift shows around the country.

Fenton Offerings

About 1985, Fenton began marketing its own assortments directly to the same dealers formerly sold by Levay. This glassware was not shown in Fenton catalogs or recorded in regular price lists. Frank Fenton recalls that the company realized that the relationship with Levay was winding down, but that Fenton still felt the offerings were viable products.

In early 1985, a Fenton color flyer announced a small assortment of "Selected Green Opalescent Blown Optics." All had the color code GO, but each item had a different optic effect: 1353 10" tulip vase, fine dot optic; 1738 5½" basket, diamond optic; 1803 3-piece fairy light, fern optic; 2007 7-piece water set, twisted drapery optic; 2323 10" double crimped bowl, double wedding ring optic; and 3138 7" basket, ribbed spiral optic.

A Fenton price sheet dated January 1, 1985, lists the Green Opalescent pieces described above, and it also lists the following eight pieces of Butterscotch Green Opalescent Carnival (G8): 8454 5" Drapery rosebowl; 9425 8" ribbon candy edge 3-footed bowl; 9435 8½" ribbon candy edge Drapery basket; 9436 rosebowl basket with looped handle; 9456 swung Drapery vase; 9540 6" Strawberry ladies stemmed cuspidor; 9542 8" Strawberry jack-in-the-pulpit vase; and 9546 6½" Strawberry footed rosebowl.

The next Fenton offering was Ruby Marble (RX), a "slag glass" effect which is similar to the Imperial Glass Corporation's Ruby Slag. Fourteen different articles were produced.

In November, 1985, Fenton made a seven piece assortment dubbed "Selected Green Opalescent with Cobalt Blue." The 9063 6" Sydenham bell and these five Thumbprint articles (all color coded GK) were made with a cobalt blue "crest" treatment added to the green opalescent glass: 4401 4-piece epergne; 4426 8" bowl; 4429 footed comport; 4438 8½" basket; and 4452 5" salt jar. The 8408 3-piece Persian Medallion fairy light (GG) was made with the shade and base in green opalescent and the candle insert in cobalt blue.

In 1988, Fenton's offerings were designated "Collector's Extravaganza." Two opalescent assortments were made in "limited production" (i. e., orders must be received by a given date). These were billed as "authentic reproductions from antique moulds—treasures of the past, pleasures for the future." The colored sheets announcing these assortments were included in the Fenton catalog mailing to regular customers. These assortments sold quite well, affirming the company's "back to basics" approach in its regular line.

The Pink Opalescent (UO) Hobnail assortment was introduced in January 1988, and expanded in May due to its strong showing in the marketplace. A Topaz Opalescent (TO) assortment was available in May 1988, but it did not sell quite as well as the Pink Opalescent.

The Collector's Extravaganza theme was continued with the 1989 Persian Blue Opalescent (XC) assortment and a 1990 assortment called Sapphire Blue Opalescent (BX), which included some items from Fenton's Gracious Touch party plan.

The Persian Blue Opalescent production (available June 1 to December 31, 1989) proved to be a very strong seller. The Sapphire Blue Opalescent (BX) production (available June 1 to December 31, 1990) was described as "authentic reproductions from antique moulds," and the color sheet billed them as "treasures of the past, pleasures for the future."

Fenton also used the Collector's Extravaganza theme for two offerings in 1991 (Stiegel Blue Opalescent and Light Amethyst Carnival), but a 1992 promotion for Persian Pearl was billed as the "Historic Collection," a designation which continued in the 1990s. Although Gary Levi continued to receive royalties from Fenton's production using his Westmoreland moulds, he last acted as a consultant to Fenton in 1992.

In addition to Fenton's production for Levay and its own similar promotions, there were other customers, notably Doris Lechler, Dorothy Taylor, and Mary Walrath (Cherished Editions).

Lechler's Heirlooms of Tomorrow

A Columbus, Ohio, kindergarten teacher, Doris Lechler authored several books on children's glass, china and furniture in the 1980s. She also edited a newsletter called "Miniature News," contributed frequently to *Glass Review*, and organized several well-attended conventions of enthusiastic collectors. Fenton made several limited edition miniature glass sets for Lechler. Although the various items were originally components of a named series ("Elizabeth," "Grace" or "Ruth"), these miniature articles can be discussed individually.

A plain custard (CT) tumble up set (7346 water carafe with 7345 tumbler) and a plain custard 8-piece lemonade set (pitcher, six tumblers and 7317 7¼" round tray) were the initial pieces made in 1980 . Later, some of each were decorated with handpainted violets (VD), and 75 lemonade sets were decorated with Christmas Holly with berries and a red bow (LH; Fenton's Louise Piper also handpainted some samples with a pansy motif). Later, Fenton's Ruby Overlay (RO) was used for the plain tumble up set; these proved difficult to produce, and only 75 sets were made.

A 7-piece lemonade set, with 7368 ruffled pitcher, was made in Burmese and decorated with the rose motif (RB); the same mould was used to produce amethyst pitchers, and 8-piece lemonade sets (pitcher, six 7345 tumblers and round tray) were made in plain amethyst (AY) as well as amethyst with two decorations—lilies of the valley (LX) or blue birds and roses (the latter, which bore code LF for "Lechler Fancy," was designed by Louise Piper and only 75 sets were made; they were advertised in the *Glass Review* for April, 1983).

A Hobnail 3361 pitcher and matching 3341 tumblers were made in Cranberry Opalescent and combined with a French Opalescent tray for a lemonade set (these could be purchased with either four or six tumblers). There was also an 8-piece set in French Opalescent (FO) as well as another in cobalt blue cased with milk glass on the inside (OK).

A Hobnail punch set (3921 one-piece punch bowl, six 3941 handled cups and 7318 round tray) was made in French Opalescent and decorated with handpainted roses and forget-me-nots (RF); the cups have a rose in the base. This same set was also made later in cobalt blue (undecorated) as well as cobalt blue with a handpainted floral motif on the inside of the punch bowl and the outside top rims of the cups.

In the fall of 1982, another small pitcher (7369) was used for a tumble up set in which the tumbler (7349) fit neatly inside the mouth of the pitcher. The set was made in a satin finished, light blue glass cased with milk glass on the inside (OU, Glacial Blue Overlay); these were satin finished with acid and decorated with handpainted flowers (LU). The same set was made in milk glass cased with cobalt blue (OK). These also have handpainted floral dec-

This ad for Lechler's Cranberry Opalescent Hobnail set appeared in the *Glass Review*.

Fenton's Topaz Opalescent (TO)

3407 . . . . Cactus water set
4801 . . . . .4-piece Diamond Lace epergne
5171 . . . . butterfly on stand
8428 . . . . Fantail bowl
8442 . . . . .3-toed nut dish
8454 . . . . .Drapery footed rose bowl
8603 . . . . .Regency table set (creamer, spooner,
covered sugar and covered butter)
9101 . . . . .24" Gone with the Wind lamp
9134 . . . . .Butterfly & Berry basket
9425 . . . . .ribbon candy edge footed bowl
9435 . . . .ribbon candy edge Drapery footed basket
9436 . . . . . . .Drapery footed rose bowl basket with
looped handle
9495 . . . . .Butterfly & Berry hat

Made in 1988, these have the Fenton logo.

Fenton's Pink Opalescent (UO) Hobnail

A3000 . . . . .pitcher and bowl set
A3308 . . . . .25" Gone with the Wind lamp
A3335 . . . . .looped handle basket
A3362 . . . . . .6½" jack in the pulpit blown vase
A3701 . . . . .10" jack in the pulpit epergne
A3712 . . . . .14-piece master punch set
A3720 . . . . . .12" pie crust crimped banana stand
A3795 . . . . .toothpick
A3801 . . . . .miniature epergne set
A3830 . . . . .10" pie crust crimped basket
A3834 . . . . .6½" basket
A3854 . . . . . . .4½" ruffled top rose bowl
A3861 . . . . .4¼" crimped rose bowl
A3863 . . . . .cruet w/stopper
A3908 . . . . .7-piece water set
A3937 . . . . .7" handled bon bon

Made in 1988, these have the Fenton logo.

note: the "A" before each number is simply Fenton's way of designating a special, i. e., not in the line, product.

Fenton's Ruby Marble (RX)

4401 . . . . .4-piece Thumbprint epergne
5151 . . . . .bear cub
5160 . . . . .fawn
5162 . . . . .bunny
5171 .butterfly on stand
5177 . . . . .Alley Cat doorstop
5186 . . . . .small hen on nest
8623 . . . . .6" Regency cupped bowl
8634 . . . . .6½" Regency basket
8635 . . . . .10" Regency basket
8680 . . . . .Regency covered butter
9027 . . . .Grape & Cable double crimped bowl
9085 . . . . .Grape & Cable cuspidor
9188 . . . . .Grape & Cable tobacco jar

Made in 1985, these have the Fenton logo.

This ad for Lechler's "Victorian" motif appeared in the *Glass Review* (April, 1983); the decoration was created by Fenton's Louise Piper.

Fenton's Persian Blue Opalescent (XC)

1353 . . . . . . .10" tulip vase, jack in the pulpit,
fine dot optic
1404 . . . . .7-piece Coin Dot water set
1413 . . . . .22" Coin Dot lamp
1435 . . . . .5" Coin Dot top hat basket
1461 . . . . .Coin Dot creamer
1492 . . . . .Coin Dot top hat
1803 . . . . .3-piece fairy light
1830 . . .5½" double crimped basket, fern optic
1865 . . . . .fern optic cruet
2323 . . . . . .10" double crimped bowl, double
wedding ring optic
3138 . . . . .7" ribbed spiral optic basket
4801 . . . . .4-piece Diamond Lace epergne
8231 . . . . .handled Multi-Fruit comport,
8-point crimp
8234 . . . . . .Persian Medallion double crimped
. . . . footed comport
8330 . . . . .7" basketweave open edged basket
with looped handle
9027 . .double crimped Grape and Cable bowl
9580 . . . . . . .Button and Arch covered butter
9638 . . . . .three-toed Grape basket,
double crimped

Made in 1989, these have the Fenton logo.

orations, and the pitcher was combined with four or six tumblers on a cobalt blue tray to form a lemonade set.

Lechler was still advertising some of the above articles in *Glass Review* as late as January-February, 1984, and some were also sold in the Fenton Gift Shop. Most of these were pictured in her *Toy Glass* (Antique Publications, 1989), where she noted that "all Lechler Heirlooms have been sold out for several years."

Taylor's Encore and MLT Glass

Dorothy Taylor of Kansas City, MO, was greatly interested in the re-issues of Carnival glass which first began to appear in the 1960s from companies such as Imperial and, later, L. G. Wright, Westmoreland, L. E. Smith, and, of course, Fenton. She published a bimonthly newsletter entitled "Carnival Glass Encore" as well as books in the *Encore by Dorothy* series, which illustrated and discussed many pieces of "new Carnival glass."

Taylor also organized several conventions for collectors, and various glass plants, including Fenton, made special souvenirs for this group. Her son, Mike Taylor, operated "MLT Glass," and Fenton made some special pieces for him, also.

At the 1980 Encore Convention, five Fenton Carnival glass Lily of the Valley pieces, signed and dated by Don Fenton were sold (see *Encore by Dorothy, Book II*, pp. 64-65). These were not special Encore pieces, but they do serve to indicate the beginning of Taylor's relationship with Fenton.

Fenton made a limited edition (500 sets) miniature God and Home pattern 7-piece water set in Red Burmuda Carnival (RN) for Taylor in 1981 (the cobalt blue Carnival version of this set had been made in 1979 for Taylor by Mosser; the moulds were made by Albert Botson of Cambridge, Ohio). Several other God and Home moulds (miniature plate, cup, saucer, sugar, creamer and covered butterdish) were also made for Taylor by Botson, and then the Mosser firm (also of Cambridge) made the glass. Incidentally, the God and Home motif was one of the great mysteries among Carnival glass collectors for quite some time, but research now points to the Dugan Glass Co. of Indiana, Pa., as the manufacturer of the full-size water set which was the inspiration for Taylor's venture in miniature.

Dorothy Taylor contracted with Westmoreland for a miniature basket in red carnival glass which was inspired by Fenton's c. 1918 Kittens motif (Botson also made this mould). Westmoreland was unable to make the baskets, so Taylor had the mould shipped to Imperial in Bellaire, Ohio, where a few samples were made. Imperial was also unable to produce the piece, so Taylor took the mould to Fenton, who made the miniature Kittens basket in 1982. These were marked "Encore, 1982, K. C. Mo." but they do not carry the Fenton logo since the mould was not owned by the company. Fenton also made the souvenir for Encore in 1983, a two-piece miniature Vintage epergne in Cobalt Carnival.

The success of the Kitten basket led Taylor to arrange for Fenton to produce a series of miniature baskets. The plans were announced in the October, 1982, issue of "Carnival Glass Encore." Taylor promised "about nine or ten baskets over a period of two or three years." These utilized the same basket mould, of course (Botson

9607 RN
7 Piece Miniature
Water Set
Pitcher measures 4¼" in height
Tumblers are 2⅛" tall

Taylor's God and Home miniature water set was limited to 500 sets.

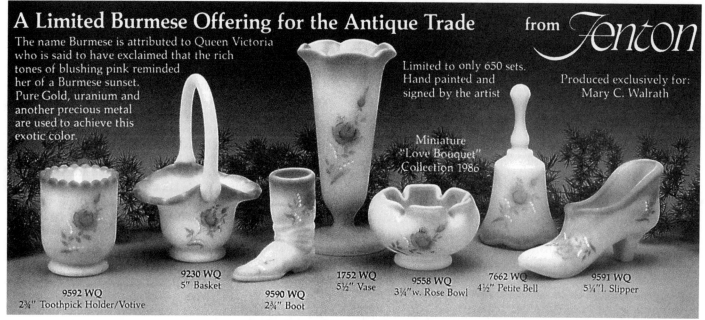

Ad for Mary Walrath's Burmese (1986).

made the different plungers), and Fenton produced these miniature baskets: Kitten (Aqua Opal, 1982); Panther (Cobalt Carnival, 1983); Pony (Vaseline Opal with pie crust edge, 1983); Detroit or Parkersburg Elk (Green Carnival, 1983); Peach Opal Farmyard (1984); Stag & Holly (Teal Blue, 1984); Dragon & Lotus (1985); Lion (1985). A contemplated Horse's Head or Horse Medallion basket was not made. Most of these motifs were based on old Fenton designs, but several (Pony and Farmyard) had their roots in the Dugan/Diamond plant at Indiana, Pa.

Mike Taylor's MLT Glass seems to have been a short-lived concern. The first pieces made for MLT Glass by Fenton in late 1981 were Peach Opalescent Carnival (PI), using the 5150 Atlantis vase mould. This mould, which was purchased by Fenton from the United States Glass Company's Glassport, Pa., plant in 1964, dates back to the 1930s, when it was designed by Robert A. May for the Duncan Miller firm in Washington, Pa. (Tony Tomazin sorted this story out in the December, 1983, issue of "Carnival Glass Encore").

Fenton's 5150 Atlantis mould was used for five MLT Glass items in Peach Opalescent Carnival: a flared version, called "hi bowl" (A); the standard vase (B); a spittoon (C); a fan vase (D); and a rose bowl (E). Fewer than 100 were made of each shape, and they retailed for $49.50 each. The color flyer which advertised these pieces called them "A Limited Offering for the New Glass Collector of America." A basket was also made, although just a few of these were produced. A few standard vases were made in Fenton's French Opalescent glass.

A letter (dated November 16, 1981) on the reverse side of the color flyer also mentioned ten different shapes in Peach Opal made from the "bottom of the Beaded Fairy Light...691 in all." Also mentioned were pieces made from a Fenton Hobnail compote mould, again in Peach Opal. This letter and color flyer were included with the December, 1981, issue of "Carnival Glass Encore," and some "whimseys made from the Peach Opal Atlantis vase" were advertised by Dorothy Taylor in this same issue. [There is little mention of MLT Glass after this time, although Dorothy Taylor occasionally advertised one of the pieces].

Walrath's Cherished Editions

In mid-1982, Fenton made an assortment of decorated Burmese for Cherished Editions, a Brownsville, New York, business, operated by Mary Walrath. Called Love Bouquet (code WQ), the assortment consisted of six items: 7235 5" basket; 7255 10" jack in the pulpit vase; 7424 4½" rose bowl; 7546 4½" vase; 7552 6½" jack in the pulpit vase; and 7558 6" bud vase. Fenton made 500 sets of the six pieces (these were signed and numbered), but unnumbered pieces could also be purchased one at a time. The floral decoration consisted of a pink rose and rosebud along with some white lily of the valley and blue forget-me-nots.

In 1986, Fenton produced another decorated Burmese assortment for Walrath. Again called Love Bouquet (code WQ), this assortment consisted of seven "miniature" items: 1752 6½" vase; 7662 petite bell; 9230 5" basket; 9558 rose bowl; 9580 boot; 9591 slipper; and 9592 toothpick holder. The seven pieces were sold only in complete sets, and Fenton made 650 sets, handpainted and signed by the artist. These were promoted by Walrath with a color sheet similar to the Levay sheets, and they were advertised in the *Glass Review* (April, 1986).

NOTES ON THE COLOR PLATES

The color pages in this book capture the breadth, depth and diversity of Fenton glass in the 1980s decade.

You will see hundreds of items from the Fenton line in a variety of colors as well as limited edition articles (Connoisseur Collection, the Artists' Series, the Designer Series or others) and offerings for occasions such as Christmas or Mother's Day. Also pictured are many special items made for QVC as well as glass collector's club souvenirs and articles made for the Levay Distributing Company.

Much of the glass pictured was drawn from Fenton's own storage archives or from displays in the Fenton Museum. Additionally, many Fenton glass collectors loaned items for the photography sessions, which required several days at the Fenton plant.

Original color transparencies from Fenton catalogs, catalog supplements and other promotional materials made it possible to include some items or treatments that would not otherwise have been available. Because these transparencies were taken for various purposes, you will notice different size characteristics and "props" (flowers, candy, etc.) appearing in a few shots.

The captions on each page identify the articles pictured and usually provide Fenton's ware numbers and color codes. Dates given generally reflect the time when the piece was first listed in a Fenton catalog or catalog supplement or was being made for a special promotion. Consult the Index in this book to locate discussions of specific items or colors in the various chapters or the locations of other illustrations.

1. Connoisseur Collection (1986) Burmese Satin 7400 SB 20" Mariner lamp with handpainted Shells motif.

2. Connoisseur Collection (1985) Burmese Satin 7602 EB 22" lamp with handpainted Butterfly and Flowering Branch motif.

3. Connoisseur Collection (1986) Burmese Satin 7666 SB bell with handpainted Shells motif.

4. Whimsey Burmese hat vase with butterfly decoration designed by Louise Piper (made for the Fenton Art Glass Collectors of America, 1982).

These items in Daisies on Cameo Satin (CD) appeared in Fenton's 1979-80 catalog.

5.   9056 CD bud vase.

6.   7488 CD temple jar.

7.   7252 CD 7" vase.

8.   7215 CD 20½" hammered colonial lamp.

9.   5166 CD frog.

10.   5197 CD happiness bird.

11.   7237 CD 7" basket.

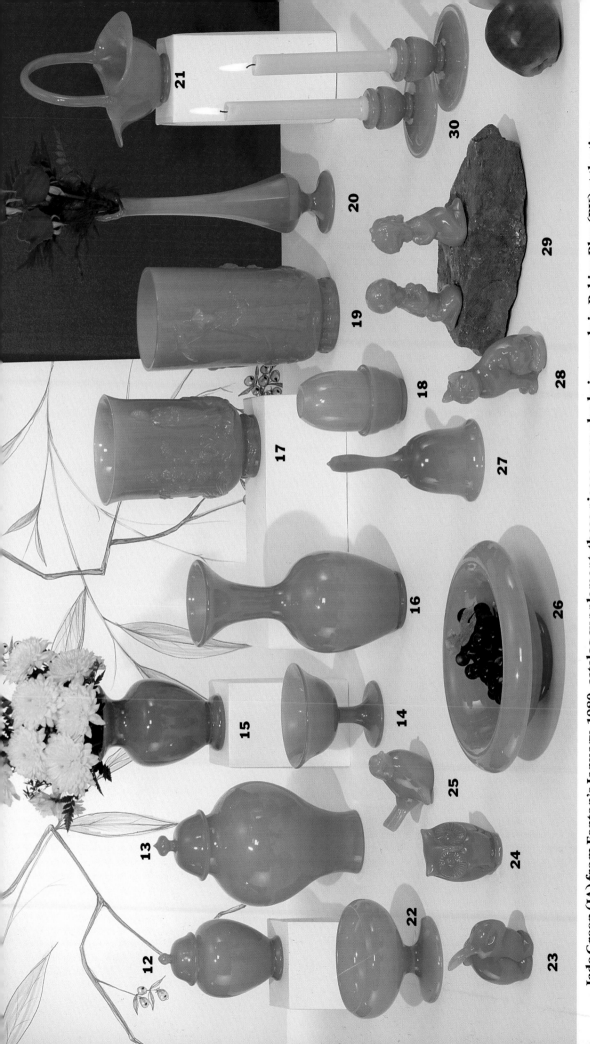

Jade Green (JA) from Fenton's January, 1980, catalog supplement; these pieces were also being made in Peking Blue (PK) at the time.

12. 7488 JA temple jar.
13. 7588 JA tall temple jar.
14. 7529 JA nut dish.
15. 7550 JA 7" vase.
16. 7557 JA 10" vase.
17. 8252 JA Empress vase.
18. 7500 JA 2-pc. fairy light.

19. 8251 JA Mandarin vase.
20. 9054 JA tall bud vase.
21. 7537 JA 7" basket.
22. 7528 JA comport.
23. 5162 JA bunny.
24. 5168 JA owl.
25. 5163 JA small bird.

26. 7523 JA rolled rim bowl.
27. 7564 JA bell.
28. 5165 JA cat.
29. 5100 JA boy and girl.
30. 7572 JA candleholders.

83

These Country Cranberry (CC) items from Fenton's January, 1982, catalog supplement were also sold by J. C. Penney stores.

31. 8528 CC 8" sphere vase.

32. 5858 CC 8" vase.

33. 2050 CC 6½" feather vase.

34. 2060 CC 70 oz. feather pitcher.

35. 2534 CC 7" daisy basket.

36. 1866 CC 16 oz. fern pitcher.

37. 7435 CC 11" basket.

38. 1824 CC 4½" fern vase.

39. 1433 CC 9½" vase.

40. 1432 CC 32 oz. coin dot pitcher.

These Silver Poppies on Ebony (PE) pieces from Fenton's 1981-1982 catalog were also sold by J. C. Penney stores.

41. 7557 PE 9½" vase.

42. 7561 PE 10¾" vase.

43. 7588 PE tall temple jar.

44. 7558 PE bud vase.

45. 7521 PE 6" bowl.

46. 7522 PE ivy ball.

47. 7488 PE small temple jar.

48. 7550 PE 6½" vase.

These handpainted Chickadee (CQ) lamps appeared in Fenton's 1981-82 catalog (the 7506 CQ hanging swag lamp and the 7507 CQ French Provincial lamp were also made).

49. 7503 CQ 23½" Rochester student lamp.
50. 7504 CQ 19" princess lamp.

A handpainted decoration, Butterflies and Bamboo (YB) appeared in Fenton's 1981-82 catalog.

51. 7504 YB 19" princess lamp (night light in lower globe).

52. 7507 YB 25¹/₂" French Provincial lamp.

These four pieces of Mountain Reflections (MV) were featured in Fenton's 1981-1982 catalog; four other items were also produced: 7257 MV 10" vase; 7419 MV 8" plate; 7503 23¹/₂" Rochester student lamp; and 7564 MV bell.

53. 7506 MV hanging swag lamp.

54. 7204 MV 16" hammered colonial lamp.

55. 7437 MV basket.

56. 7300 MV 2-pc. fairy light.

57

58

59

These "oil well scenic" (OW) lamps were created by
Michael Dickinson in 1981. They were marketed
with a special mailing to customers in the Texas-
Oklahoma area.

57. 7508 OW 22" lamp.

58. 7204 OW 16" hammered colonial lamp.

59. 7510 OW 20" lamp.

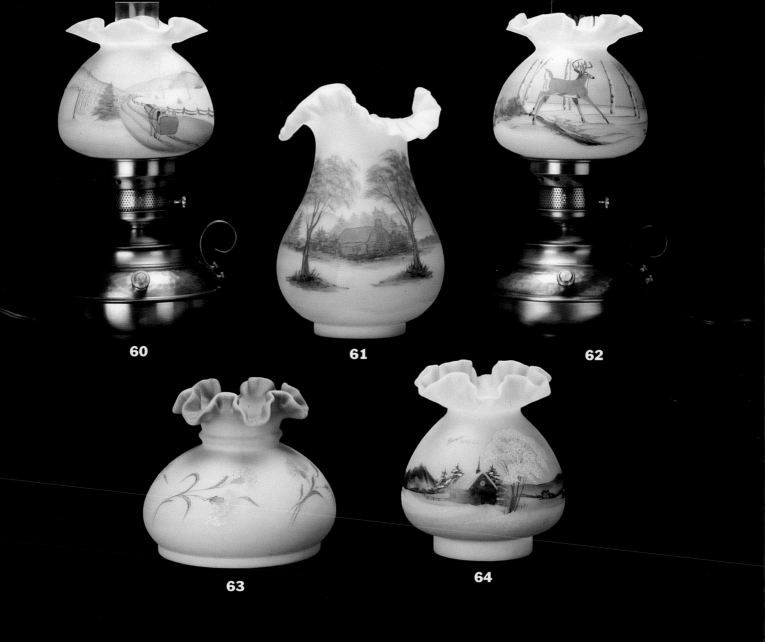

60. 7204 GH 16" hammered colonial lamp (this motif, called Going Home, was designed by Diane Johnson and was part of the Christmas Classics Series in 1980).

61. 7215 LC shade, Log Cabin on Custard Satin (this is probably a sample; note the blue coloration in the sky).

62. Designer Series (1985) 7204 DW Nature's Grace 16" hammered colonial lamp.

63. Iced Carnations Burmese shade (this sample was designed by Louise Piper).

64. 7204 CV shade (production sample of designer Mike Dickinson's Christmas Morn for the 1978 Christmas Classics Series).

These Strawberries on French Opalescent (SF) items were put in the Fenton line in 1980 or 1981.

65. 7229 SF nut dish.

66. 9056 SF bud vase.

67. 7429 SF comport.

68. 9356 SF bud vase.

69. 6056 SF 6" vase.

70. 9334 SF Basketweave 7" basket.

71. 9305 SF Basketweave 20" Student lamp.

72. 9320 SF Basketweave 4½" vase.

73. 9304 SF 2-pc. fairy light.

74. 5165 SF cat.

75. 9462 SF Basketweave bell.

76. 5163 SF small bird.

77. 5169 SF duckling.

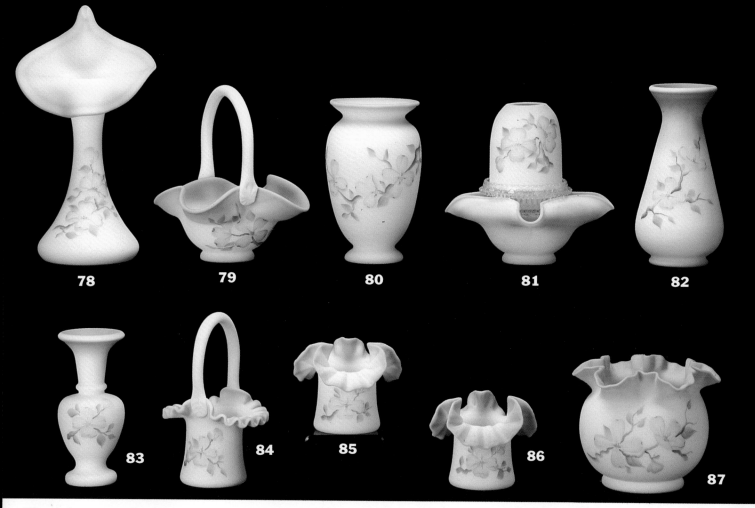

The Pink Dogwood on Burmese Satin (PD) pieces shown on this page were made about 1981.

78. 7255 PD 10½" tulip vase.

79. 7535 PD 7½" basket.

80. 7560 PD 6½" vase.

81. 7501 PD 3 pc. fairy light.

82. 7559 PD 7½" vase.

83. 7558 PD 6" vase.

84. 7235 PD 6" basket.

85 - 86. 7442 PD 5" vases (note the different coloration on the rims).

87. 7547 PD 5½" vase.

The Love Bouquet (WQ) decoration on Fenton's Burmese was first developed for Mary Walrath's Cherished Editions enterprise in 1982, and some WQ miniature items were also made for her about four years later.

88. 1752 WQ 5½" vase (1986).

89. 9591 WQ slipper (1986).

90. 9590 WQ boot (1986).

91. 7546 PD 4½" vase.

92. 9558 WQ rose bowl (1982).

93. 9592 WQ toothpick holder (1986).

94. 7552 PD 6¾" small tulip vase.

95.   96.   97.   98.   99.

100.   101.   102.   103.   104.

105.   106.   107.   108.   109.   110.   111.

After a limited offering of Velva Rose (VR) proved popular in 1980, both Velva Rose and Velva Blue (VB) were in Fenton's 1981-1982 catalog. The Pink Velvet, Blue Velvet and Crystal Velvet items in the bottom row were made later, as noted.

95. 9455 VR 9" handkerchief vase.

96. 9488 VB candy box.

97. 8405 VR beaded fairy light.

98. 9128 VB Sheffield 7½" shallow bonbon.

99. 9432 VR 11" Panelled basket.

100. 8250 VR miniature rose bowl.

101. 8431 VR Water Lily comport.

102. 7562 VB star crimped bell.

103. 9423 VR 6" Floral bouquet vase.

104. 9422 VB Persian Medallion comport.

105. Barnyard Buddies (1985) V1774 V4 lamb bell.

106. Barnyard Buddies (1985) V1774 V5 goose bell.

107. Barnyard Buddies (1985) V1774 V3 piglets bell.

Items 108-111 were in the Prayer Children group introduced in January, 1984.

108. Pink Velvet 9662 VP girl bell.

109. Blue Velvet 9648 VK boy mug.

110. Pink Velvet 9605 VP girl light.

111. Crystal Velvet 9662 VE girl bell.

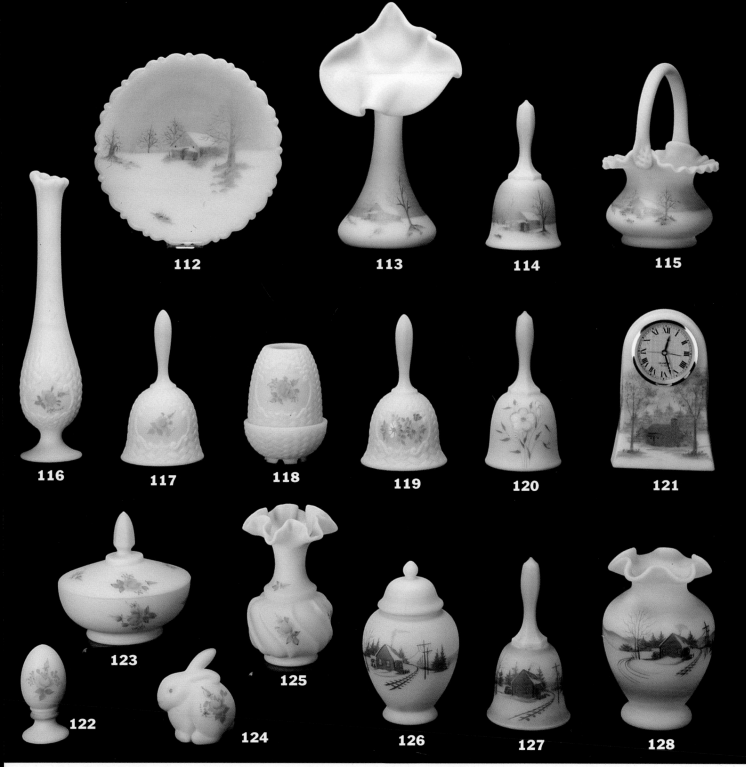

112

113

114

115

116

117

118

119

120

121

123

122

124

125

126

127

128

Sunset on Cameo Satin (SS) appears in Fenton's 1981-1982 catalog along with Chocolate Roses on Cameo Satin (DR) and Daisies on Cameo Satin (CD). Designer Mike Dickinson's Down by the Station (TT) was produced in 1983.

112. 7418 SS 8" plate.

113. 7255 SS 10³/₄" large tulip vase.

114. 7564 SS bell.

115. 7437 SS 7¹/₄" basket.

116. 9356 DR Basketweave bud vase.

117. 9462 DR Basketweave bell.

118. 9304 DR Basketweave fairy light.

119. 9462 CD Basketweave bell.

120. Wildflowers 7564 FD bell (1983).

121. Log Cabin 8600 LC clock.

122. 5140 DR egg on stand.

123. 7484 DR candy box.

124. 5162 DR bunny.

125. 6056 DR Wave Crest vase.

126. 7488 TT temple jar.

127. 7564 TT bell.

128. 7530 TT 6¹/₂" vase.

In 1981, Fenton's Nativity Scene items were made in Antique Blue (TB), Antique Green (TG), Crystal Velvet (VE), Florentine Brown (FL) and Florentine Blue (FT).

129. 9463 FT nativity bell.

130. 9412 FT nativity plate.

131. 9401 FT nativity fairy light.

132. 9412 VE nativity plate.

133. 9463 VE nativity bell.

134. 9401 VE nativity fairy light.

135. 9412 FL nativity plate.

136. 9401 FL nativity fairy light.

137. 9463 FL nativity bell.

138. 9412 TG nativity plate.

139. 9463 TG nativity bell.

140. 9401 TG nativity fairy light.

141. 9463 TB nativity bell.

142. 9412 TB nativity plate.

143. 9401 TB nativity fairy light.

Forget-Me-Not Blue (KL) was introduced in January, 1982.

144. 6370 KL Flower Band candleholders.

145. 6320 KL Flower Band 9" bowl.

146. 6321 Flower Band nut dish.

147. 6380 Flower Band large comport.

148. Christmas in America Series 8281 FL 8" plate (San Xavier del Bac, 1981).

149. Currier & Ives Series 8417 TN plate (Harvest, 1981).

150. Currier & Ives Series 8415 TB plate (The Old Homestead in Winter, 1982).

151. Nativity 9412 FT plate (1981).

152. Special order 7418 8" plate for the Minerva, Ohio, sesquicentennial in 1983.

153. Designer Series (1983) Lighthouse Point on Custard Satin 7418 LT 8" plate (created by Mike Dickinson).

154. Designer Series (1983) Down Home on Custard Satin 7418 FV 8" plate (created by Gloria Finn).

155-156. Designer Series (1984) Smoke and Cinders on White Satin 7667 TL bell and 7618 TL plate (created by Mike Dickinson).

157-158. Designer Series (1984) Majestic Flight on White Satin 7618 EE plate and 7667 EE bell (created by Beverly Cumberledge).

159-160. Mandarin 8251 HU vase and Empress 8252 HU vase, Blue on Cameo Satin (also made in HI, Ivory on Cameo Satin).

161. Mountain Reflections 7257 MV 10" vase.

The Iris Collection (IN) on Bone White was produced in 1982.

162. 7557 IN 9" vase.

163. 7564 IN bell.

164. 7559 IN 7¹/₂" vase.

165. 7539 IN 7¹/₂" basket.

166. 7550 IN 6¹/₂" vase.

167. 7521 IN 6" bowl.

Petite Fleur (PF) on opaline glass appeared in Fenton's January, 1984, catalog supplement.

168. 7544 PF 5" vase.

169. 7573 PF Melon candleholder.

170. 7549 PF Melon bowl.

171. 7573 PF Melon candleholder.

Blue Garland on Custard Satin (BA) appeared in Fenton's January, 1982, catalog supplement.

172. 7431 GA footed comport.

173. 7488 GA temple jar.

174. 7564 GA bell.

175. 7534 GA 7" basket.

176. 7241 GA 4½" vase.

177. 7530 GA 6½" vase.

Blue Dogwood on Cameo Satin (BD) was in the line from 1980-1982.

178. 9334 BD Basketweave basket.

179. 9462 BD Basketweave bell.

180. 5162 BD bunny.

181. 7229 BD nut dish.

182. 7252 BD 7" vase.

183. 9056 BD 8" bud vase.

184. 5163 BD bird.

185. 7564 BD bell.

186. 7363 BD handled bottle.

187. 7488 BD temple jar.

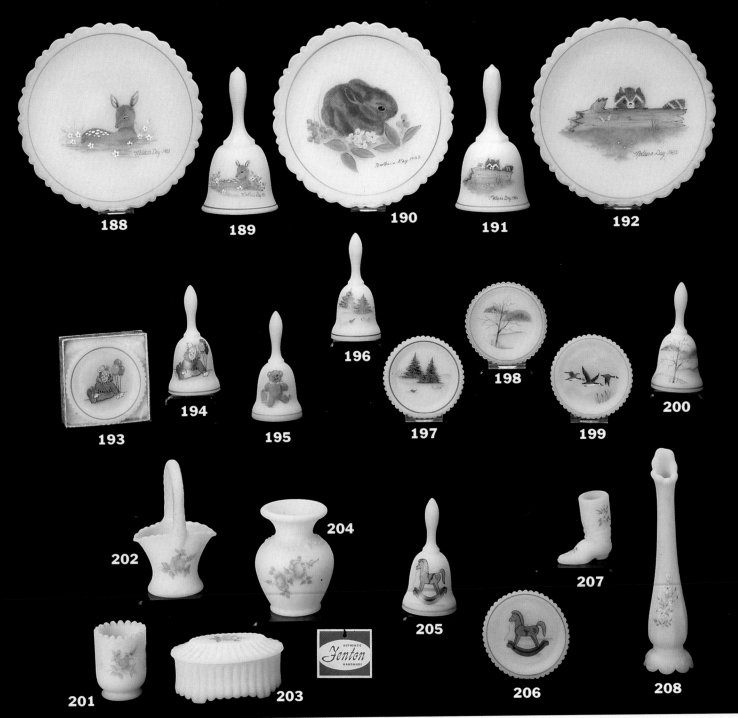

188-189. Mother's Day Series (1981) Gentle Fawn on Custard Satin 7418 FN 8" plate and 7564 FN bell.

190-191. Mother's Day Series (1982) Nature's Awakening on Custard Satin 7418 NA 8" plate and 7564 NA bell.

192. Mother's Day Series (1983) Where's Mom on Custard Satin 7418 RQ 8" plate.

193-194. Childhood Treasures Series (1985) Clown on Custard Satin 7615 CL cup plate and 1760 CL petite bell.

195. Childhood Treasures Series (1983) Teddy Bear on Custard Satin 1760 TE petite bell.

196-197. Artists' Series (1982) After the Snow on Custard Satin 1760 TC petite bell and 7615 TC cup plate.

198. Artists' Series (1983) Winter Chapel on Custard Satin 7615 WC cup plate.

199. Artists' Series (1985) Flying Geese on Custard Satin 7615 FG cup plate.

200. Artists' Series (1983) Winter Chapel on Custard Satin 1760 WC petite bell.

Blue Roses on Custard Satin (BQ) was made in 1981.

201. 9592 BQ toothpick.

202. 9536 BQ basket.

203. 9589 BQ oval jewel box.

204. 7554 BQ 5" vase.

205-206. Childhood Treasures Series (1985) Hobby Horse on Custard Satin 1760 HQ petite bell and 7615 HQ cup plate.

207-208. Pink Blossom on Custard Satin 9590 PY boot and 9556 PY 8½" bud vase (both made in 1981).

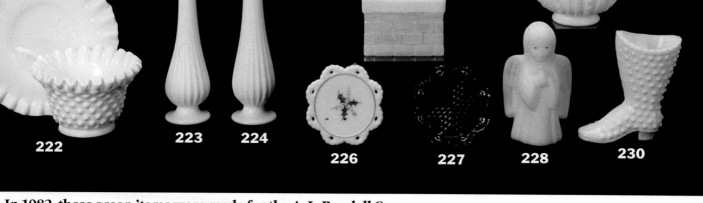

In 1982, these green items were made for the A. L. Randall Co.

209. R9457 GS Faberge 7" ribbed vase.

210. R9430 GS 6" Water Lily bowl.

211. R8430 GS Water Lily footed bowl.

212. R9426 GS Faberge 4¹/₂" ribbed bowl.

213. R9451 GS Faberge 6" ribbed bud vases (pr.).

214. 9780 RU ruby Heart comport, 1989.

215. 9557 RU ruby votive, 1986.

216-217. 1714 RU ruby ornament and 1714 KG green ornament, 1982.

218. 9763 RU ruby Heart petite bell.

219. 1760 RD handpainted white roses petite bell, 1988.

220 - 221. R9426 RU 4¹/₂" Faberge ribbed bowl and R9430 RU 6" bowl, both made for the A. L. Randall Co. in 1982.

222. 3803 MI 3-pc. mayonnaise set, 1981-82.

223-224. R9451 MI Faberge 7" ribbed vases.

225. Santa in Chimney 5235 DS (Opal Carnival handpainted, 1988).

226-227. Handpainted Christmas ornaments 1714 DH and 1714 CY (1982).

228. Praying Angel 5114 AB (Opal Satin w/blue highlights, 1985).

229. R9426 MI 4¹/₂" ribbed bowl (made for the A. L. Randall Co. in 1982).

230. Milk Glass Hobnail 3992 MI 4" boot, 1981-82.

**Christmas Fantasy Series
(1985-86) Heart's Desire WP**

231. 7667 WP bell.

232. 7418 WP 8" plate.

233. 7300 WP 2-pc. candlelight.

231

232

233

235

234

234. Christmas Fantasy Series (1983) Anticipation 7418 AI 8"
plate AI 1983.

235. 7669 VZ musical (plays "Joy to the World") bell with
Christmas message (1988).

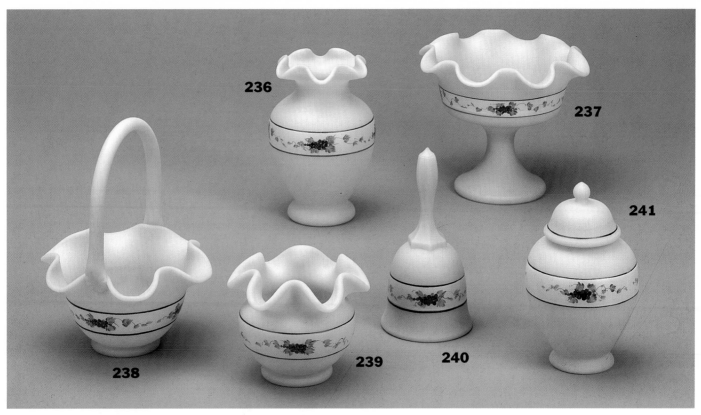

The Vintage (VI) decoration was produced in 1982 on Cameo Satin glass.

236. 7530 VI 6$\frac{1}{2}$" vase.

237. 7431 VI footed comport.

238. 7534 VI 7" basket.

239. 7241 VI 4$\frac{1}{2}$" vase.

240. 7564 VI bell.

241. 7488 VI temple jar.

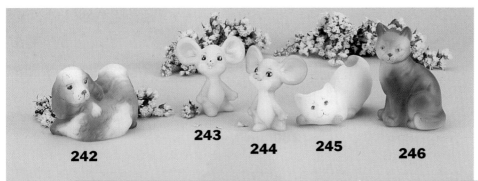

The Natural Animals occupied a prominent place in Fenton's 1985-86 Classic catalog.

242. 5159 SP spaniel.	**246.** 5165 NG gray cat.	**250.** 5163 NY yellow small bird.
243. 5148 NG gray mouse.	**247.** 5151 PJ panda.	**251.** 5147 NM drake mallard.
244. 5148 NJ brown mouse.	**248.** 5160 NF fawn.	**252.** 5147 NQ blue wing teal duck.
245. 5119 NX kitten.	**249.** 5163 NO orange small bird.	**253.** 5147 ND canvasback duck.

264   265   266   267   268

269   270   271

272   273

Except as indicated, most of these pieces are from Fenton's January, 1982, catalog supplement and the Sculptured Ice Optics offering.

264. 8552 AY 9$\frac{1}{2}$" vase.

265. 8551 AY 10$\frac{1}{2}$" cylinder vase.

266. 8553 AY 6$\frac{1}{2}$" vase.

267. 8550 AY 10" vase.

268. 8560 AY 70 oz. pitcher.

269. 7582 AY Dolphin comport.

270. 8520 BB 12" Glacial Blue bowl.

271. 7580 AY Dolphin jar.

272-273. Jacqueline 9139 MG 10$\frac{1}{2}$" basket and Jacqueline 9442 MG 9$\frac{1}{2}$" bowl in Mulberry (MG), made about 1989.

274 **275** **276** **277**

278 **279** **280**

281 **282** **283** **284**

274 and 277. Sophisticated Ladies sandcarved on Ebony 7561 SX vase and 7651 SX vase, both made in 1982.

275. Azure Blue Satin vase (made for Avon's Gallery Originals in 1984).

276. 7661 MD Mother and Child 9" vase, sculptured Rose Velvet (Connoisseur Collection, 1984).

278. 1796 BY 7¼" Blossoms and Bows on Cranberry vase (Connoisseur Collection, 1987).

279. 8812 EK Silhouettes on Ebony 10½" vase, made in 1986.

280. 9486 QY Enameled Azure pitcher (Connoisseur Collection, 1987).

281 and 284. Silver Poppies on Ebony 7522 PE ivy ball and 7561 PE 10¾" vase, both made about 1981.

282. Iris sandcarved on Amethyst 7559 IY vase, 1982.

283. 9054 RD Roses on Ruby bud vase, 1981.

285–286. Strawberry 9454 RT Country Peach 10" bud vases, 1982.

287. Basketweave 9626 PH Sunset Peach comport (designed by Peter Yenawine).

288. This twisted cane (milk glass, ruby and crystal) was made in 1984 and sold through the Gift Shop.

289–290. (Connoisseur Collection , 1984) 3134 PV Plated Amberina Velvet 10" basket and 3193 PV top hat (the 5090 PV cane matching the top hat is shown in Fenton's May, 1984, catalog supplement).

291–292. Country Peach 8248 RT Scroll & Eye comport and 7582 RT Dolphin handled vase, both from 1982.

293. Salem Blue 8625 SR Puritan comport, c. 1990.

294. Craftsman 9660 bell in green iridescent, probably a sample made about 1982.

295. Cameo Opalescent 8450 CO Lily of the Valley handkerchief vase, 1981.

296, 297 and 299. Inspirations line 8740 II blue iceberg, 8741 IH pink iceberg, and 8741 II blue iceberg (1988).

298. Misty Morn 8741 MM handpainted iceberg (1988).

300. Christmas Faith 7667 XS bell (designed by Louise Piper, 1986).

301. Flower Band 6371 KL Forget-Me-Not Blue ashtray c. 1982.

302. Butterfly & Berry 9134 HG 7" basket in Heritage Green, c. 1983.

All of these Katja/Fenton USA items were made in 1982-83.

303. K7753 KC large blown vase with Blue fade effect.

304. K7724 KO 9³/₄" bowl with Flame banded effect.

305. K7763 KO large bottle with Flame banded effect.

306. K7762 KO medium bottle with Flame banded effect.

307. K7764 KE small bottle with Aquamarine rim.

308. K7754 KE small blown vase with Aquamarine rim.

309. K7743 KN small cylinder with Hickory spiral effect.

310. K7743 KN small cylinder with Hickory spiral effect.

311. Sample fine rib optic vase with Flame (KO) rim.

312. K7751 KE small bottle with Aquamarine fade effect.

313. Sample fine rib optic vase with Flame (KO) rim.

314. K7761 KN small bottle with Hickory banded effect.

315. K7761 KO small bottle with Flame banded effect.

316. K7761 KO small bottle with Flame banded effect.

These two pages show items in Amethyst (AY), Candleglow (YL) Federal Blue (FB), and Heritage Green (HG) from An American Legacy, Fenton's 1982-83 line.

317. G1652 YL 10" vase.

318-319. G1660 AY 70 oz. pitcher and G1660 HG 70 oz. pitcher (note the slightly different handles).

320. G1625 FB 11" oval bowl.

321-322. G1603 sugar and cream set.

323. G1692 YL sugar shaker.

324. G1665 HG bell.

325. G1645 YL goblet.

326-327. G1606 AY salt and pepper set.

These two pages show items in Amethyst (AY), Candleglow (YL) Federal Blue (FB), and Heritage Green (HG) from An American Legacy, Fenton's 1982-83 line.

328. G1678 AY decanter with stopper.

329-330. G9071 YL candleholders.

331. G1652 FB 10" vase.

332. G1636 FB basket.

333. G1645 HG goblet.

334. G1625 AY 11" oval bowl.

335. G1618 AY 8" oval relish.

336. G1674 YL cruet with stopper.

337. G1692 AY sugar shaker.

338. G1644 YL wine.

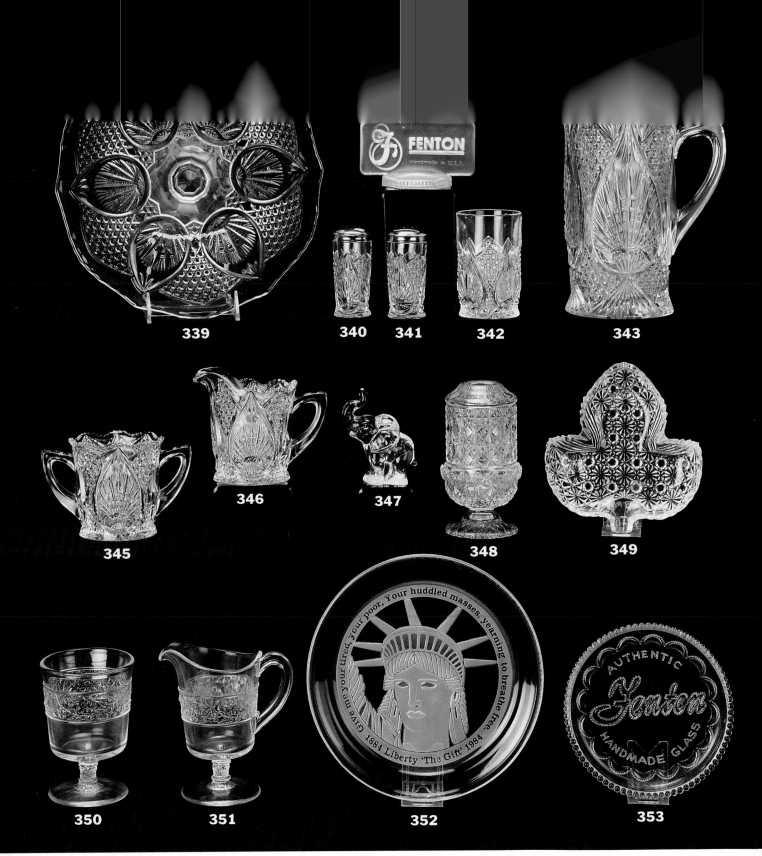

339-343. Regency 8613 CY footed cakeplate, 8606 CY salt & pepper, 8644CY tumbler and 8664CY pitcher, all made c. 1983.

344. Fenton logo 9799 FO in French Opalescent, c. 1986.

345-346. Regency 8602 CY sugar and creamer set.

347. 5158 CY elephant (1986-87).

348. Fine Cut & Block 9102 CY 2 pc. fairy light (1981).

349. Daisy & Button 1976 CY leaf tray (1981).

350-351. Flower Band 6300 CY sugar and creamer set (1982).

352. Statue of Liberty 8011 LE 9" plate, sandcarved on crystal (Designer Series, 1985).

353. Fenton logo plate in crystal experimental, c. 1981.

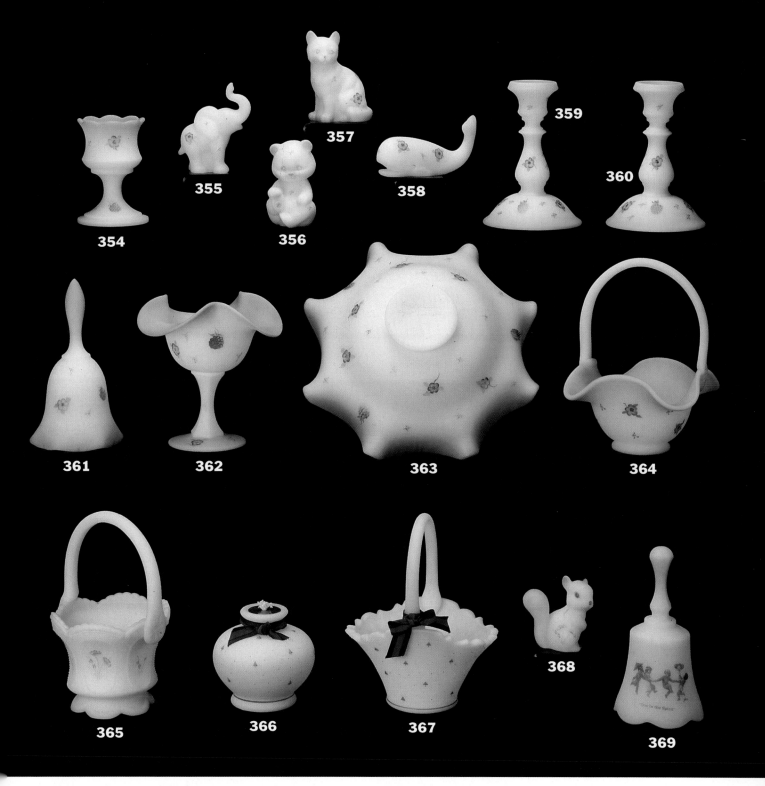

Fenton's Berries and Blossoms on Opal Satin (RK) was quite popular in 1984-85.

354. 7275 RK footed votive.

355. 5158 RK elephant.

356. 5151 RK bear.

357. 5165 RK cat.

358. 5152 RK whale.

359-360. 7475 RK candlesticks.

361. 1773 RK bell.

362. 1628 RK comport.

363. 7622 RK 9" bowl.

364. 7635 RK 7" basket.

365 and 368. Meadow Blooms on Opal Satin 9639 JU 7¹/₂" basket and 5215 JU squirrel (1986).

366-367. Winter on Opal Satin 7609 XT oil lamp and 8637 XT oval basket (1985).

369. This Opal Satin sample 7669 bell has the One in the Spirit motif.

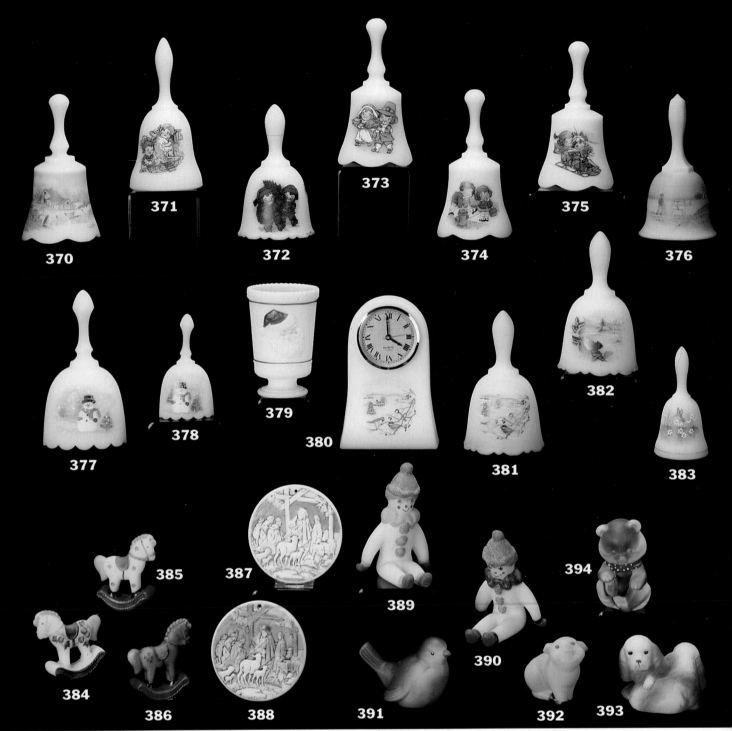

370. Country Scene on Opal Satin 7668 LT bell.

371-375. These Campbell Kids Collection (1985) bells were padprinted on Custard Satin:

371. 7668 K2 Summer Fun bell.

372. 7668 K6 Christmas Cheer bell.

373. 7668 K5 Thanksgiving Joy bell.

374. 7668 K3 Back to School bell.

375. 7668 K4 Winter Wonderland bell.

376. Special order 7564 bell, hand-painted on Cameo Satin for the Schaller, Iowa, centennial, 1983.

377-378. Snowman (1985) on Opal Satin 7673 SM musical bell and 7674 SM musical petite bell.

379. Santa (1985) on Opal Satin 9673 XN votive.

380-381. Birds of Winter Series (1988), A Chickadee Ballet on Opal Satin 8600 BD clock and 7668 BD bell.

382. Birds of Winter Series (1987) Cardinal in the Churchyard on Opal Satin 7668 BC bell.

383. Artist's Series (1986) "The Hummingbird" on Custard Satin 1760 HW petite bell.

384-386. 5135 BQ Winterberry hobby horse (1988), 5135 Spotted Horse on Opal Satin (made as sample in 1985), and 5135 HY Brown Horse on Opal Satin (1985).

387-388. Antique Brown nativity 9414 TD ornament (1982) and Florentine nativity 9414 FL ornament (1982).

389-390. 5111 NE Blue Clown on Opal Satin and 5111 NL Red Clown on Opal Satin (both made in 1985).

391-393. These are from Fenton's Natural Animals (1985-86) group: 5163 NO robin, 5220 QP pig, and 5159 SP spaniel.

394. French Opalescent Valentine's Day 5151 FO bear with bow (1986).

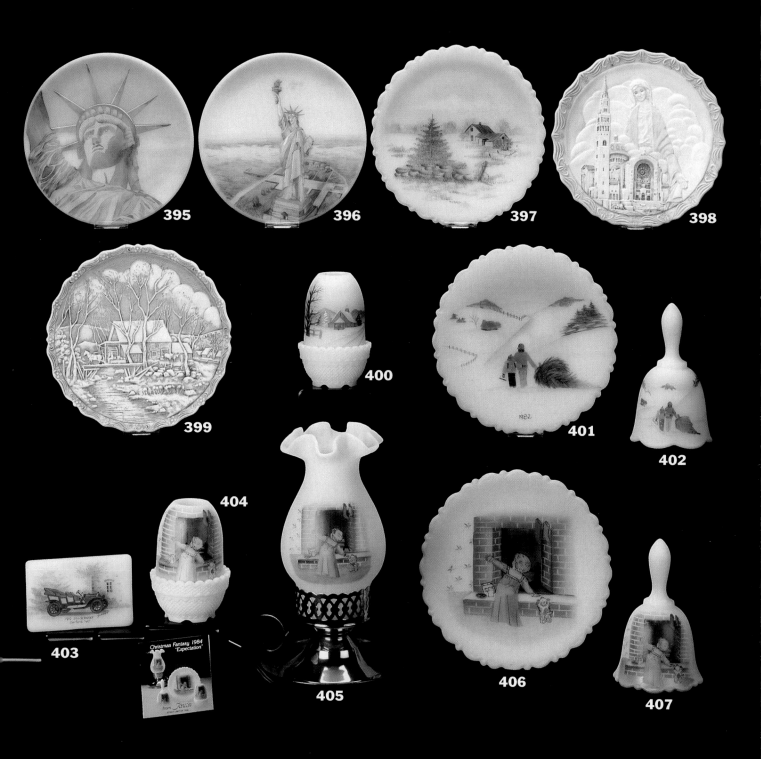

395. Designer Series (1986) Statue of Liberty 7618 L6 8" plate.

396. Designer Series (1985) Statue of Liberty 7618 LO 8" plate.

397. Country Scene 7418 LT 8" plate (1989-90).

398. National Shrine of the Immaculate Conception special order plate.

399. Currier and Ives Series (1981) Winter in the Country Antique Blue 8418 TB 8" plate.

400. Christmas Classics Series (1981) All is Calm 7300 AC fairy light.

401-402. Christmas Classic Series (1982) Country Christmas 7418 OC 8" plate and 7466 OC bell.

403. American Classic Series (1986) Studebaker 7698 SU desk plaque.

404-407. Christmas Fantasy Series Expectation 7300 GE fairy light, 7512 GE hurricane lamp, 7418 GE 8" plate and 7667 GE bell (all 1984).

408 **409** **410** **411**

412 **413** **414** **415** **416**

417 **418** **419** **420** **421** **422** **423**

During the mid-1980s, Fenton began to introduce new groups of Carnival glass which stayed in the line about a year. Unless otherwise indicated, these items are Cobalt Marigold Carnival (NK).

408. 9461 NK Plytec 32 oz. pitcher (1987).

409. 9728 NK Acanthus bowl (1987).

410. 9614 NK Garden of Eden 8" plate (1985).

411. Sunburst 8667 NK pitcher (1985).

412. Sample Favrene Orange Tree candlestick.

413. 8654 NK vase (1984).

414. 9637 NK Leaf with Butterfly basket (1985).

415. Sunburst 8636 CN basket (amethyst Carnival, 1983).

416. 9234 NK Butterfly and Berry basket (1986).

417. 5134 NK snail (1985).

418. 5226 NK fox.

419. 9292 NK Button and Arch votive/toothpick holder (1986).

420. Currier and Ives Series (1984) Winter in the Country amethyst Carnival 8418 CN plate.

421. 9663 NK Garden of Eden bell (1985).

422. Connoisseur Collection (1984) Ruby Carnival 9163 UR Famous Women bell.

423. Coaster for the Australian Carnival Glass Enthusiasts.

424. Spiral Optic Melon 3140 OP vase in Periwinkle Blue Overlay (1985).

425. Dogwood 9650 OP 11" vase in Periwinkle Blue Overlay (1985).

426. Wheat 5858 OP vase in Periwinkle Blue Overlay (1985).

427. 3106 OF lamp in Federal Blue Overlay (1983).

428. Dogwood 9658 OP 8" vase in Periwinkle Blue Overlay (1985).

429. Pearly Sentiments on Opal Carnival 9539 PT basket with porcelain rose (1989).

430. Connoisseur Collection (1988) iridescent Teal cased 3132 OT Melon basket.

431. Antique Rose 7630 AF Aurora 7" basket (1989).

432. Connoisseur Collection (1985) 3712 GO Green Opalescent Hobnail punch bowl with base.

433. 3847 GO punch cups.

434. Connoisseur Collection (1985) 4809 GO Green Opalescent Diamond Lace 4-pc. epergne.

435. Paneled Daisy 9185 PE Shell Pink covered candy (1989).

436. Shell Pink Butterfly covered box (made for the Fenton Art Glass Collectors of America in 1988).

437. 5228 PE Shell Pink Doll (made for the Gracious Touch party plan).

438. Country Cranberry 8551 CC 10¹/₂" cylinder vase (1982).

439. Sculptured Ice Optics Glacial Blue 8551 BB 10¹/₂" cylinder vase.

440. Country Cranberry 1353 CC fine dot optic 10" tulip vase (1989).

441. Country Cranberry 1552 CC rib optic 10¹/₂" urn vase (1988).

442. Country Cranberry 1432 CC Coin Dot optic pitcher (1982).

443. Connoisseur Collection (1988) handpainted Cranberry 6080 ZX Wave Crest covered candy box.

444. Lilac 9666 LX Sandwich pattern pitcher (1990).

445. Country Cranberry 5838 CC basket (made for the Gracious Touch party plan).

446. Connoisseur Collection (1983) Vasa Murrhina 6432 IM melon basket.

447. Connoisseur Collection (1988) handpainted Wisteria 7666 ZW bell.

448. Connoisseur Collection (1983) Vasa Murrhina 6462 IM cruet.

449. Country Cranberry 9434 CC Jacqueline basket (1989).

117

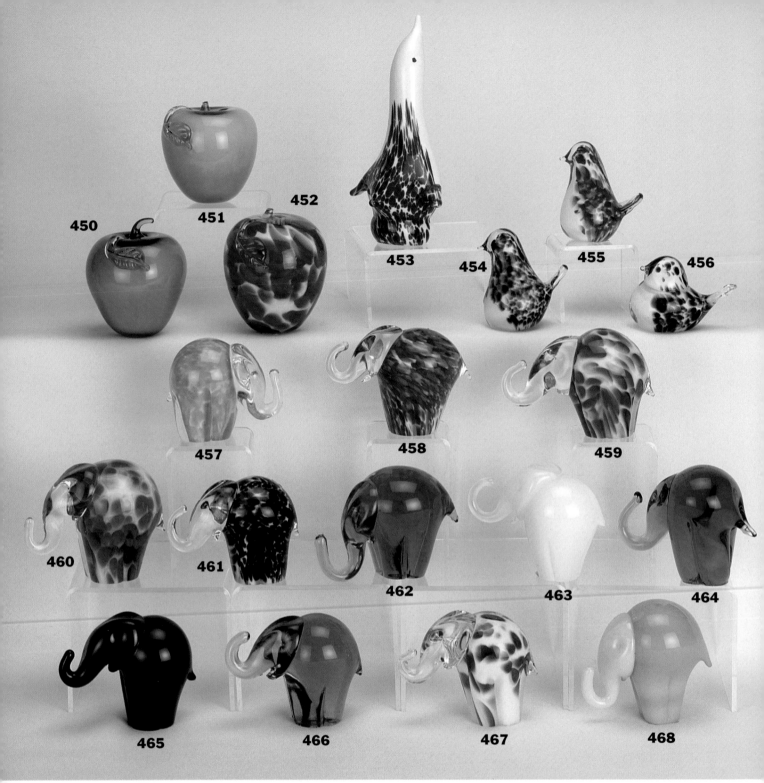

450 **451** **452** **453** **454** **455** **456** **457** **458** **459** **460** **461** **462** **463** **464** **465** **466** **467** **468**

These off hand items were produced by glassworker Delmer Stowasser, who retired from the Fenton plant in 1990. Some of the multi-colored animals, made using various colors of frit, were sold through the Fenton Gift Shop in 1984; others are experimental or "one-of-a-kind."

450-451. Federal Blue 5019 OF apple and Dusty Rose Overlay 5019 OD apple (regular Fenton line in 1984).

452. Apple made with cranberry frit (a gift to Tina Ferrell in 1990).

453. 5014 penguin (1984).

454-456. 5011 birds in various colors (sold in Fenton Gift Shop, 1984).

457-461. 5012 elephants (sold in Fenton Gift Shop, 1984).

462. Experimental pink elephant, 1980.

463. Experimental opal elephant, 1980.

464. Experimental blue/gray elephant, 1980.

465. Experimental black elephant, probably 1980.

466. Experimental "smoke" elephant (1980).

467. 5012 elephant (sold in Fenton Gift Shop, 1984).

468. Experimental Blue Burmese elephant (1980).

469

470

471

472

473

474

475

476

477

478

479

The Blue Ridge (BI) items were part of Fenton's special 80th anniversary assortment in 1985. The "Almost Heaven" Blue Slag (a name coined by Bill Fenton) items in the bottom row were sold during the Fenton Gift Shop's annual February sale in 1989.

469. 2632 BI basket.

470. 2640 FO tumbler.

471. 2664 BI pitcher.

472. 2603 BI lamp.

473. 2635 BI basket.

474. 2624 BI large bowl.

475. 2604 3-pc. fairy light (the insert is crystal).

476. "Almost Heaven" Blue Slag 3674 candleholder.

477. "Almost Heaven" Blue Slag 3674 candleholder.

478. "Almost Heaven" Blue Slag 9188 Grape and Cable tobacco jar.

479. "Almost Heaven" Blue Slag 5228 doll.

All of these are from the 1985 Artisan Series called Geometrics, which was created by Richard Delaney using a combination of etching and polishing. The colors are Gray (EG), Periwinkle (EP) and Rose (ER). Several other Geometrics are also on the next page.

480. 8802 ER 12" h. oval vase.

481. 8801 ER 12" d. oval vase.

482. 8802 EG 12" h. oval vase.

483. 8807 EP 9" vase.

484. 8805 ER 6" vase.

485. 8806 ER 7¹/₂" vase.

486. 8811 ER 8" "V" shaped bowl.

487. 8810 ER 9" shallow bowl.

488. 8810 EP 9" shallow bowl. **489.** 8809 EP 6¼" oil candle. **490.** 8811 EP 8" "V" shaped bowl.

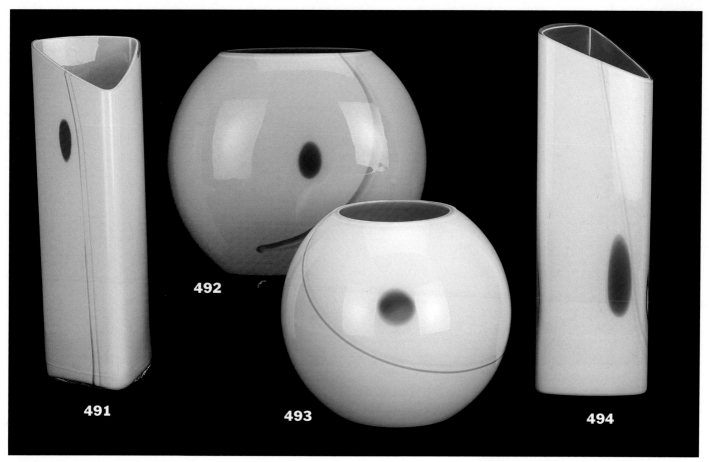

These items are from the 1985 Artisan Series Masterworks Collection. They were designed by glassworker Delmer Stowasser.

491. 8803 UV triangle vase 15" h.
492. 8801 NV oval vase 12" d.

493. 8804 KM sphere vase 10" d.
494. 8803 KM triangle vase 15" h.

495 496 497 498

499 500 501 502 503

505 507

504 506 508 509 509 510

Unless otherwise indicated, these items are Crystal (CY) or Crystal Velvet (VE).

495. 9259 VE Spring 8¾" vase (Verlys mould, 1987).

496-497. Connoisseur Collection (1983) White Satin Carnival 9660 WI Craftsman Bell and 9640 WI Craftsman stein.

498. 8252 VE Empress vase (possibly a sample, 1987).

499. 9761 VE Cross bell (1989).

500-501. Faberge 9451 VE Faberge 7" bud vase and 9431 VE miniature basket (1981-82).

502. Prayer Children 9649 VE girl mug (1984).

503. 9782 VE Daisy comport (1987).

504. 5214 CY scottie (1986).

505. 5148 FO mouse in French Opalescent (1986).

506. 5215 VE squirrel (1986).

507. 5160 VE fawn (1985).

508. 5159 VE spaniels (1981).

509. 5101 VE Kissing Kids (1981).

510. 8691 VE desk clock (1988).

511. Connoisseur Collection (1984) handpainted Rose Velvet 9651 HD 9" vase.

512. Connoisseur Collection (1983) Sculptured Rose Quartz 7659 GJ 7" vase.

513. Connoisseur Collection (1989) Rosalene 7605 RE 5-pc. epergne.

514. Burmese 8257 BR Peacock 8" vase (1987-88).

515. Connoisseur Collection (1989) Vasa Murrhina 6453 RG pinch vase.

516. Connoisseur Collection (1984) Embossed Swan 9458 AV Gold Azure vase.

517. Connoisseur Collection (1983) Sculptured Rose Quartz 7542 FJ 4¹/₂" oval vase.

518. Connoisseur Collection (1988) cased French Opalescent and ruby with teal ring iridized 2556 ZI 6" tulip vase.

519. Burmese iridized 5150 Atlantis vase (sold in a Collector's Room sale, 1991 or 1992).

520. Connoisseur Collection/85th Anniversary offering sample Tulip vase with raspberry decoration (1990).

521. Sample 5531 Empress decorated pitcher (1990).

522. 7235 WQ Burmese 5" basket (made for Mary Walrath, 1982).

523. Connoisseur Collection (1984) Blue Burmese satin 9394 UE 3-pc. covered candy box.

524. Sample decorated Burmese basket (probably for Mary Walrath, 1986).

525. Burmese ruffled pitcher with handpainted roses (made for Doris Lechler, 1986).

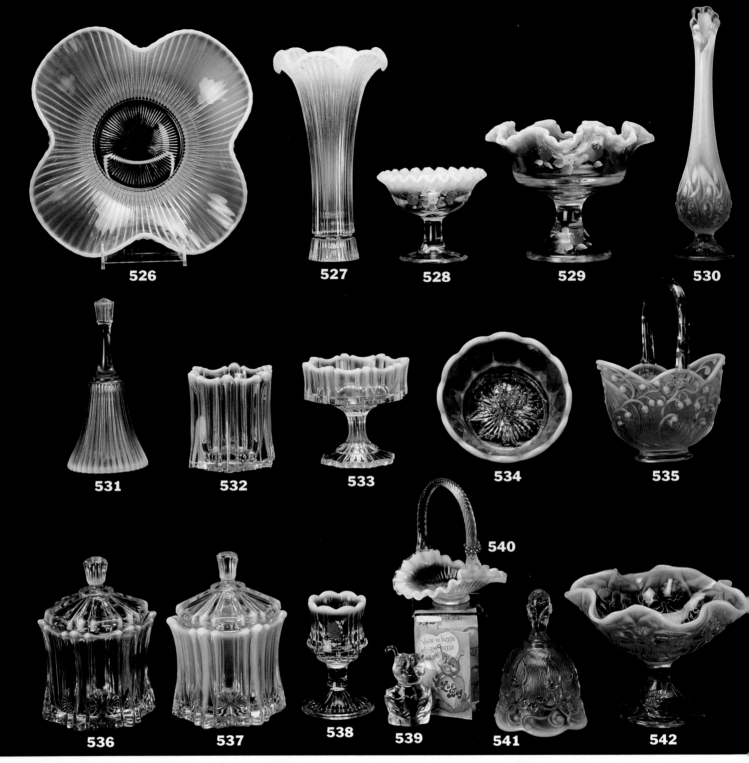

526. Reflections (Sheffield) 6625 UO Peaches and Cream 11" bowl (1986).

527. Reflections (Sheffield) 6654 EO Minted Cream 11" (1986).

528-529. Strawberries on French Opalescent 9229 SF nut dish and 7429 SF 6" comport (1981).

530. Lily of the Valley 8458 BO Blue Opalescent 11" bud vase (1981).

531. Reflections (Sheffield) 6665 UO Peaches and Cream bell.

532. 9555 EO Minted Cream votive (1986).

533. French Opalescent 9571 FO footed nut dish (1986).

534. 8225 BO Grape nappy in Blue Opalescent (1981-82).

535. Lily of the Valley 8437 BO Blue Opalescent basket (1981).

536-537. 9551 UO Peaches and Cream and 9551 EO Minted Cream covered candy boxes (1986).

538. French Opalescent 7675 KR footed votive (1986-87).

539. Luv Bug 5149 CY with original box (1985).

540. French Opalescent 9535 FO basket (1986-87).

541. Lily of the Valley 8265 BO Blue Opalescent bell (1981).

542. Water Lily 8431 BO Blue Opalescent 5" comport (1979).

124

543. 3104 BI 4-pc. Blue Ridge vanity set.

544. 3194 ZS French Cranberry 13" handled urn.

545. French Royale 3190 KF 7" handled vase.

546. Teal and Milk Overlay 7438 JD top hat basket.

547. Danielle 8812 JY 10½" vase.

548. Misty Morning 8812 ET handpainted 10½" vase.

Pastel Violets (VC) appears in Fenton's 1987-88 catalog.

549. 9308 VC 23" student lamp.	**553.** 7635 VC square basket.	**557.** 5151 VC bear cub.
550. 7668 VC bell.	**554.** 7254 VC 4½" vase.	**558.** 5119 VC kitten.
551. 7660 VC ribbed vase.	**555.** 1628 VC comport.	**559.** 5148 VC mouse.
552. 5225 VC puppy.	**556.** 9056 VC bud vase.	**560.** 7662 VC petite bell.

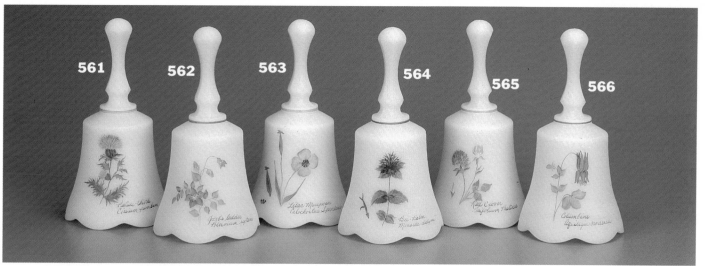

The Botanical Bell assortment (0263 AS) in Fenton's 1987-88 consisted of six 7668 bells, each handpainted with a different flower (both the common name and the Latin name appear on the bells).

561. 7668 bell (Pasture-thistle). **563.** 7668 bell (Lilac Mariposa). **565.** 7668 bell (Red Clover).

562. 7668 bell (Jacob's ladder). **564.** 7668 bell (Bee-Balm). **566.** 7668 bell (Columbine).

This assortment features Provincial Blue Opalescent (OO) and handpainted Provincial Bouquet (FS) items (1987-88).

567. 8335 OO open edge basket. **573.** 7662 FS petite bell. **579.** 8294 OO Panelled Daisy votive.

568. 9284 OO Rose ftd. cov. candy. **574.** 2057 OO 7" curtain vase. **580.** 9531 OO Strawberry nut dish.

569. 7635 FS square basket. **575.** 9519 OO heart candy. **581.** 9665 OO Beauty bell.

570. 8304 OO Valencia trinket box. **576.** 8376 OO Valencia hurricane. **582.** 5151 FS bear cub.

571. 7668 FS bell. **577.** 8323 OO open edge bowl. **583.** 1628 FS comport.

572. 9223 OO Rose footed comport. **578.** 5119 FS kitten. **584.** 5127 OO open swan.

Milk Glass (MI) Hobnail and Colonial Amber (CA) items from Fenton's 1987-88 catalog.

585. 3660 MI pitcher.

586. 3033 MI heart candy.

587. 3067 MI Wave Hobnail bell.

588. 3937 MI 2-handled bon bon.

589. 3634 MI oval basket.

590. 3022 MI Wave Hobnail rose bowl.

591. 3032 MI Wave Hobnail basket.

592. 3991 MI hat.

593. 3920 MI footed comport.

594. 3680 MI covered cookie jar.

595. 7638 CA Aurora basket.

596. 1995 CA Daisy & Button slipper.

597. 9280 CA Butterfly candy box.

598. 8294 CA votive.

599. 3952 CA Hobnail vase.

600. 7620 CA Aurora vase.

601. 5197 CA happiness bird.

602. 9667 CA Aurora bell.

603. 8327 CA Valencia nut dish or soap dish.

604. 8356 CA Valencia bud vase.

Periwinkle Blue (PW) items from Fenton's 1986-87 catalog and Peaches 'n Cream (UO) items from the 1987-88 catalog.

605. 9652 PW Beauty vase.

606. 9627 PW Beauty bowl.

607. 9665 PW Beauty bell.

608. 9626 PW Basket Weave comport.

609. 8371 PW Barred Oval votive.

610. 1995 PW Daisy & Button slipper.

611. 5171 PW butterfly on stand.

612. 9144 PW Fine Cut & Block ring-holder.

613. 7275 PW votive.

614. 8321 PW Barred Oval 6½" bowl.

615. 8333 PW Barred Oval 6" basket.

616. 8351 PW Barred Oval 8½" bud vase.

These items are sometimes called the "new Sheffield" pattern.

617. 6655 UO votive.

618. 6625 UO bowl.

619. 6672 UO candleholders (pr.).

620. 6654 UO 11" vase.

621. 6634 UO 7" basket.

622. 6665 UO bell.

623. 6688 UO covered candy.

624. 6650 UO 6" bud vase.

625. 6626 5½" bowl.

673. Rosalene 9560 RE templebells bell (sold in Collector's Room sale, early 1990s).

674. Shell Pink 9480 PE Chessie candy box (1990).

675. Connoisseur Collection (1989) Rosalene Satin 9667 KT hand-painted bell with blue bird.

676. Connoisseur Collection (1983) Burmese Satin 7562 UF hand-painted bell.

677-678. Victorian Roses 8691 VJ clock and 9639 VJ Panelled basket (1987).

679-682. Handpainted Tulips 5780 TL heart box, 5169 TL duckling, 6322 TL Flower Band comport, and 5165 TL cat (1990).

683. Q7580 UD Dolphin handled candy dish with handpainted decoration (made for Gracious Touch party plan).

684. Sample 5140 handpainted blue roses on custard egg.

685. Pearly Sentiments 5780 PT heart box (1988).

686-688. Winterberry 9056 BQ bud vase, 9639 BQ Paneled basket, and 5160 BQ fawn (1987).

689. Pink Blossom 7596 PY picture frame (1983-84).

690. Holly Berry 5233 HL reclining bear (1988).

691. Special order 7564 bell, hand-painted on Cameo Satin for the Schaller, Iowa, centennial, 1983.

692. 85th Anniversary Collection (1990) Burmese Satin 7700 QH tumbler with handpainted Raspberry decoration.

693. Special order 5151 NC Desert Storm Schwarz Bear (1991).

134

These items in Fenton's copper Rose (KP) decoration were put into the line in 1989-91.

694-697. 9372 KP candlesticks, 7523 KP rolled rim bowl, 6322 KP Flower Band comport, and 8817 KP 8½" vase.

698-704. 7696 KP 7½" vase, 7630 KP Aurora basket, 5240 KP open bird, 5151 KP bear, 5165 KP cat, 9295 KP slipper, and 7348 KP 6" vase.

705 and 708. Handpainted Elizabeth decoration on Blue Royale 9071 EM candlestick and 6780 EM Paisley covered candy (1990).

706. Thumbprint 4469 LK Cobalt Blue ashtray with sand-carved lovebirds (1983).

707. Blue Royale 5241 KK lion (1990).

Country Scene (LT) appears in Fenton's 1990-91 catalog.

709. 7254 LT 4½" vase.

710. 7237 LT basket.

711. 7418 LT 8" plate.

712. 8600 LT alarm clock.

713. 7204 LT 16" lamp.

714. 7209 LT 21" Student lamp.

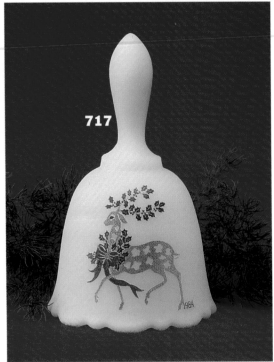

The Childhood Treasures Series (1987) Frisky Pup (PN) was designed by Dianna Barbour.

715. 1760 PN petite bell.

716. 7615 PN cup plate.

717. Designed by Yale and Frances Forman, this Reindeer Legacy sample bell was made in 1983, but it was not put into the Fenton line.

718-719. Childhood Treasures Series (1989) A child's Cuddly Friend (CX) 7615 CX cup plate and 1760 CX petite bell.

720-721. Artists' Series (1989) Househunting (AC) 1760 AC petite bell and 7615 AC cup plate.

722-723. Artists' Series (1987) Out in the Country (SF) 7615 SF cup plate and 1760 SF petite bell.

724-725. Mother's Day (1990) 7418 SN 8" plate and 7668 SN bell with handpainted swan.

Hearts and Flowers (FH) from 1990-91 catalog.

726-730. 9357 FH 4" Basketweave vase, 5148 FH mouse, 6322 FH Flower Band comport, 9252 FH 6¹/₂" Rose vase, and 9335 FH Basketweave basket.

731-737. 5151 FH bear cub, 5197 FH happiness bird, 5233 FH reclining bear cub, 5165 FH cat, 9462 FH Basketweave bell, 9589 FH oval trinket box, and 7662 FH petite bell.

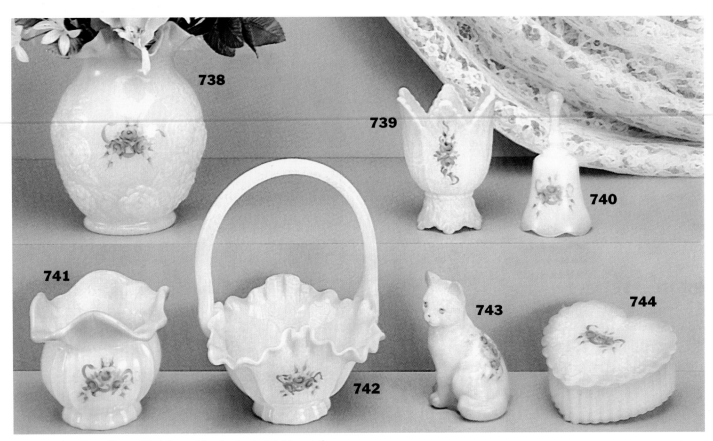

Antique Rose (AF) from Fenton's 1990-91 catalog.

738-740. 9252 AF 6¹/₂" Rose vase, 9578 AF 2-way Leaf votive, and 7662 AF petite bell.

741-744. 7620 5" AF Aurora vase, 7630 AF Aurora 7" basket, 5165 AF cat, and 5780 AF Rose heart box.

Rose Corsage (MP) from Fenton's January, 1989, catalog supplement.

745-747. 7691 MP Aurora 7" vase, 9056 MP 9¼" bud vase, and 9239 MP Panelled basket.

748-752. 8324 MP open edge comport, 9384 MP Floral trinket box, 8376 MP hurricane candle, 8267 MP Medallion bell, and 9357 MP Basketweave vase.

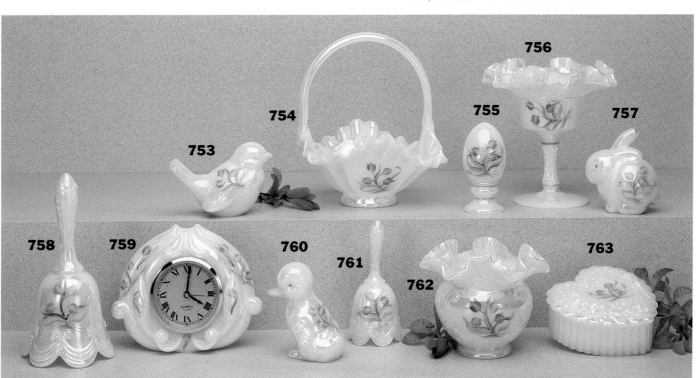

Tulips (TL) from Fenton's 1990-91 catalog.

753-757. 5163 TL bird, 7630 TL Aurora basket, 5140 TL egg, 6322 TL Flower Band comport, and 5162 TL bunny.

758-763. 9268 TL Bow & Drape 6" bell, 8691 TL alarm clock, 5169 TL duckling, 9266 TL Bow & Drape 4½" bell, 9357 TL Basketweave vase, and 5780 TL Rose heart box.

139

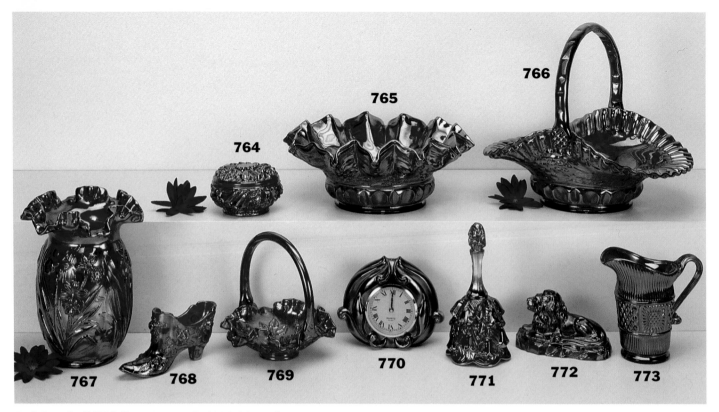

Red Carnival (RN) from Fenton's 1990-91 catalog.

764-766. 9384 RN Floral trinket box, 9059 RN 10½" Grape and Cable bowl, and 9074 RN Grape and Cable basket.

767-773. 9752 RN daffodil vase, 9295 RN Rose slipper, 9240 RN Rose basket, 8691 RN alarm clock, 9560 RN Templebells bell, 5241 RN lion, and 9666 RN Sandwich pitcher.

Teal Marigold (OI) from Fenton's January, 1989 catalog supplement.

774-777. 8227 OI Pinwheel comport, 8464 OI water Lily 36 oz. pitcher, 5127 OI open swan, and 9137 OI Fine Cut and Block basket.

778-782. 5165 OI cat, 4801 OI 4-pc. epergne, 1990 OI Daisy & Button boot, 8406 OI Heart fairy light, and 8283 OI Orange Tree and Cherry 10" bowl.

Salem Blue (SR) from Fenton's 1990-91 catalog.

783-787. 5197 SR happiness bird, 5151 SR bear cub, 8625 SR Puritan comport, 7620 SR Aurora vase, and 9544 SR Vulcan basket.

788-793. 9036 SR Priscilla 12" basket, 9266 SR Bow & Drape 4½" ball, 6780 SR Paisley covered candy box, 5243 SR cat, 8342 SR Valencia basket, and 8691 SR alarm clock.

Lilac (LX) articles from Fenton's 1990-91 catalog.

794-797. 5197 LX happiness bird, 6780 LX Paisley covered candy box, 9237 LX Rose 7¼" basket, and 9666 LX Sandwich pitcher.

798-803. 9754 LX vase with bow, 5243 LX cat, 9560 LX Templebells bell, 8691 LX alarm clock, 9266 LX Bow & Drape petite bell, and 9295 LX Rose slipper.

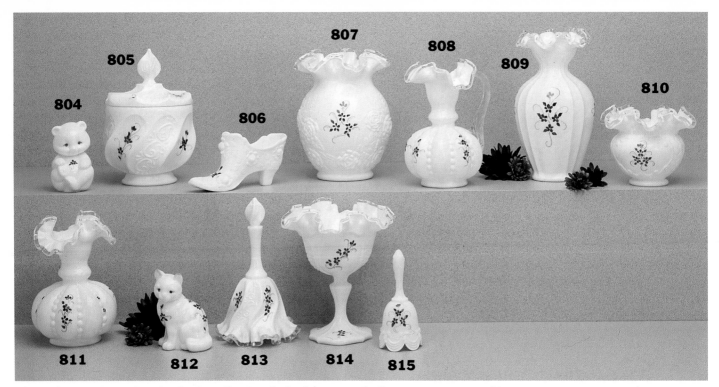

This selection from the Elizabeth Collection (ES) of decorated Silver Crest appeared in Fenton's 1990-91 catalog.

804-810. 5151 ES bear cub, 6780 ES Paisley covered candy box, 9295 ES Rose slipper, 9252 ES 6½" Rose vase, 7692 ES Beaded Melon pitcher, 7694 Aurora 7" vase, and 9357 ES Basketweave vase.

811-815. 7693 ES Beaded Melon 6" vase, 5165 ES cat, 6761 ES Paisley bell, 9229 ES Empress bell, and 9266 Bow & Drape 4½" bell.

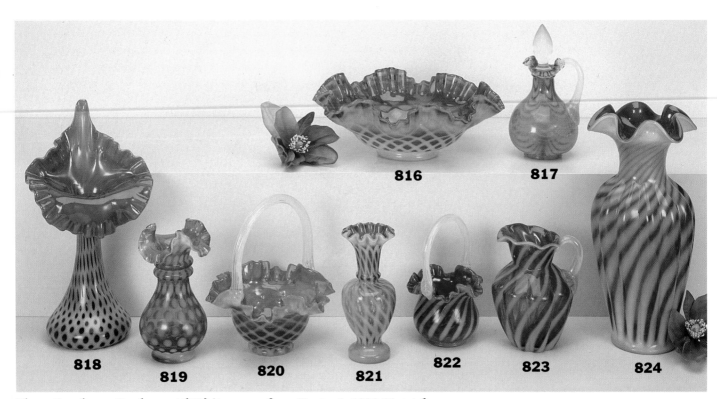

These Cranberry Opalescent (CR) items are from Fenton's 1990-91 catalog.

816-817. 1726 CR Diamond Optic bowl and 2095 CR Drapery Optic cruet with stopper.

818-824. 1353 CR Fine Dot 10" tulip vase, 1354 CR Dot Optic 7" vase, 1739 CR Diamond Optic 7" basket, 1799 CR Diamond Optic 6" vase, 3133 CR Spiral 6" basket, 3163 CR Spiral pitcher and 3161 CR Spiral 11" vase.

Dusty Rose (DK) was among the best-selling Fenton colors during the 1980s.

These Dusty Rose items appeared in Fenton's 1986-87 catalog.

825-831. 9626 DK Basketweave comport, 9531 DK Strawberry nut dish, 9433 DK Strawberry basket, 5171 DK butterfly on stand, 5186 DK hen on nest, 1995 DK daisy & Button slipper, and 7273 DK footed votive.

832-840. 9454 DK Strawberry 11½" bud vase, 9537 DK Strawberry basket, 9451 DK Faberge bud vase, 9144 DK Fine Cut & Block ringholder, 9120 DK Fine Cut & Block comport, 9280 DK butterfly covered candy box, 8466 DK Faberge bell, 9157 DK Fine Cut & Block vase, and 9659 DK vase.

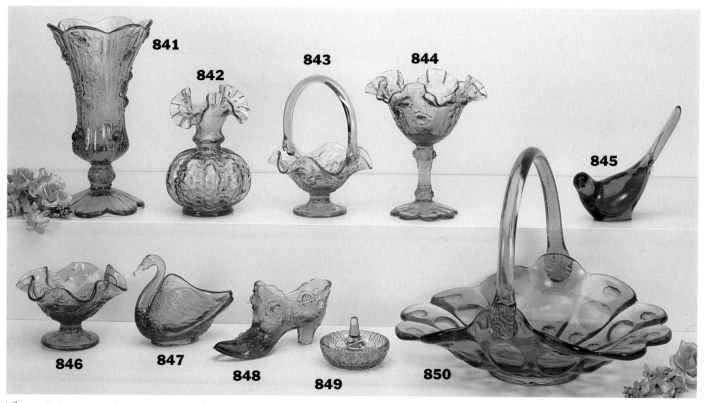

These Dusty Rose items appeared in Fenton's 1990-91 catalog.

841-845. 5750 DK Rose 9" vase, 2557 DK Beaded Melon vase, 9537 DK Strawberry footed basket, 9223 DK Rose comport, and 5197 DK happiness bird.

846-850. 9531 DK Strawberry nut dish, 5127 DK open swan, 9295 DK Rose slipper, 9144 DK Fine Cut & Block ringholder, and 9036 DK Priscilla 12" basket.

Two new colors—Cranberry Opaline (KH) and Cased Jade Opaline (AG)—were shown for the first time in Fenton's June, 1990, catalog supplement.

846. 7373 KH tulip bud vase.
847. 7727 KH 14" bowl.

848. 7371 KH 7" vase.
849. 7372 KH 13" vase.
850. 8354 KH Basket Weave 9" vase.

851. 7373 AG tulip bud vase.
852. 8354 AG Basket Weave 9" vase.

853. 7371 AG 7" vase.
854. 7372 AG 13" vase.
855. 7727 AG 14" bowl.

Fenton's Birds of Winter Series ran from 1987 through 1990. Shown here are the 1989 and 1990 offerings: Downy Woodpecker—Chiseled Song (BL) and A Bluebird in Snowfall (NB).

(at left)

856. 8600 NB 6" clock.

857. 7209 NB 21" Student lamp.

858. 7300 NB fairy light.

859. 7418 NB 8" plate.

860. 7667 NB bell.

(below)

861. 8600 BL 6" clock.

862. 7300 BL fairy light.

863. 7418 BL 8" plate.

864. 7667 BL bell.

865. 7204 BL 16" hammered colonial lamp.

866. Deep Plum Opalescent Hobnail 3720 PO pie crust crimped banana stand (made for Levay, 1984).

867. Iridized Plum Opalescent Butterfly bon bon, made for the Fenton Art Glass Collectors of America in 1982-83.

868. Iridized Plum Opalescent 9425 IP ribbon candy edge 8" bowl (made for Levay, 1984).

869. Deep Plum Opalescent Hobnail 3323 PO 4½" crimped vase (made for Levay, 1984).

870. Deep Plum Opalescent Hobnail 3804 PO 3-pc. fairy light (made for Levay, 1984).

871-872. 9188 DK and 9188 RE tobacco jars in Dusty Rose and Rosalene (these were sold during the February, 1990 Fenton Gift Shop sale).

873-874. Dianthus on Custard 7488 DN temple jar and 7534 DN basket.

875-880. The Farm (1985): 7437 F7 basket, 7530 F7 6½" vase, 8600 F8 clock, 1760 F4 mini bell, 7564 F8 bell, and 7204 F5 hammered colonial lamp (note that the lamp depicts the entire farm scene, while the others focus on a single element of the overall design, such as the well).

881-882. Mother's Day Series (1980) New Born 7564 NB bell and matching 7418 NB plate.

883. American Classic Series (1986) Jupiter 7418 TP 8" plate.

884. Special order for Bob Evans Farms 7488 EF temple jar.

885-888. Frosted Asters on Blue Satin (1983-1984): 1760 FA mini bell, 5158 FA elephant, 5152 FA whale, and 9504 FA Basketweave candlelight.

889. American Classic Series (1986) Jupiter 7514 TP 23" lamp.

890. Mother's Day Series (1983) Where's Mom 7564 RQ bell.

891. Heritage Green Overlay 1850 OH 7½" vase (1983).

892. Childhood Treasures Series (1983) 1760 TE Teddy Bear mini bell.

893. Christmas Faith 7300 XS fairy light (1986).

894. Childhood Treasures Series (1987) 7615 PN Frisky Pup cup plate.

895. American Classic Series (1986) Jupiter 7698 TP desk plaque.

896. Deer Scene 8600 PG clock (1989).

897. Budweiser Clydesdales 7564 XA bell (1983).

898. 5160 IK fawn (this was part of the True Blue Friends group in 1986).

899. Thistles and Bows 5160 EW fawn (1986).

900. Provincial Bouquet 5160 FS fawn (1987).

901. Autumn Leaves 5160 LB fawn (1985).

902. Peach Meadow Blooms 5160 PZ fawn (1985).

903. Special order lamp, "Wild Turkey Federation of America" designed by Beverly Cumberledge (1987).

904

906

904. Designer Series (1984) Smoke and Cinders 7514 TL 23" Student lamp (created by Michael Dickinson).

905. Marietta College lamp (created by Michael Dickinson).

906. Special order 7514 B8 Knights of the Sea 23" lamp.

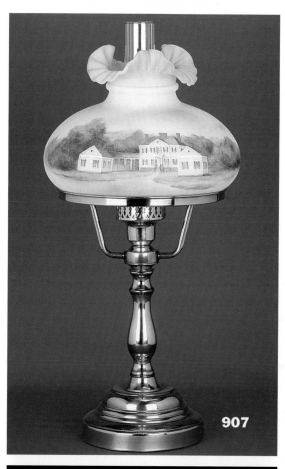

907

909

908

907. Parkersburg Bicentennial 7507 N6 25½" lamp (created by Michael Dickinson, this depicts Blennerhassett Mansion).

908. Fenton family home lamp (by Michael Dickinson).

909. Marietta Bicentennial 7503 P5 lamp (by Michael Dickinson, this depicts the "Landing of the Pioneers" oil painting by Sala Bosworth).

Fenton's May, 1990, catalog supplement announced the "85th Anniversary Offering" of these handpainted Burmese items. Each piece says "Fenton 85th Anniversary" along with the individual artist's signature and the year "1990."

910. 7731 QH Burmese 7" basket with raspberries.

911. 7412 QH Burmese 21" Student lamp with raspberries.

912. 7700 QH Burmese 7-pc. water set with raspberries.

913. 9308 RB Burmese 20" classic lamp with roses.

914. 7202 QJ Burmese 2-pc. epergne with Petite Floral.

915. 7701 QJ Burmese cruet and stopper with Petite Floral.

916. 7792 QD Burmese 9" vase with Trees Scene.

917. 7732 QD Burmese basket with Trees Scene.

918. 7791 RB Burmese 6½" vase with roses.

919. 7790 RB Burmese 6" fan vase with roses.

These items were made by Fenton for QVC (in Fenton's system, all QVC ware numbers are preceded by the letter "C").

920-921. C3360 DO Hobnail pitcher and C3938 DO Hobnail bowl, Dusty Rose Carnival with Teal crest and handle (sold as C3000 DO set in 1989).

922. CV021 8T Mulberry 11" spiral vase (Don Fenton signature, 1992), sold with black base.

923. C1353 BX Fine Dot 10" tulip vase, Sapphire Blue Opalescent (1989).

924. C8428 XB Butterfly and Berry footed bowl, Black Carnival glass (1989).

925. C3524 TX Spanish Lace bowl, Teal with Milk Glass crest (sold with C3570 TX Spanish Lace candleholders, 1988).

926. C8625 XB Puritan comport, Black Carnival glass (1990).

927. CV007 8C 3-pc. Cranberry Opalescent ginger jar, hand-painted decoration, with black lid and base (1992).

928. C8654 GZ Pinwheel vase, Holiday Green Carnival glass (1990).

929. C9560 GZ Templebells bell, Holiday Green Carnival glass (1990).

930-931. Hobnail tumbler and pitcher from 3008 XB 7-pc. water set, Black Carnival glass (1990).

932. C8335 XB Basketweave basket, Black Carnival glass (1990).

933 **934** **935** **936** **937**

938 **939** **940** **941**

942 **943** **944** **945** **946**

These items were made by Fenton for QVC (in Fenton's system, all QVC ware numbers are preceded by the letter "C").

933. C7666 KP bell, black with handpainted Copper Rose (1990).

934. C3522 TC Spanish Lace comport, White Carnival glass with Teal crest (1988).

935. C1844 CR Cranberry Opalescent fern optic vase (Bill Fenton signature, 1990).

936. C3538 TC Spanish Lace basket, White Carnival glass with Teal crest (1988).

937. C1868 XN Melon basket, Ocean Blue with Cobalt blue crest and handle (1990).

938. C5838 LU Corn Shock basket, Lilac Carnival glass (1989).

939. C9134 OM Butterfly & Berry basket, Teal Carnival with Milk Glass crest and handle (1988).

940. C9452 MG Mulberry Jacqueline vase (1990).

941. C9134 DN Butterfly & Berry basket, Dusty Rose Carnival glass with Milk Glass crest and handle (Bill Fenton signature, 1989).

942. C1866 XN Fern pitcher, Ocean Blue Opalescent with Cobalt Blue crest and handle (1990).

943. C9268 ET Easter bell, Peach Velvet with handpainted floral (1990).

944. C3570 TX Spanish Lace candleholders, Teal with Milk Glass crest (sold with C3524 TX Spanish Lace bowl, 1988).

945. C5165 KP cat, black with handpainted Copper Rose (1991).

946. C9388 RN candy box with cover, Ruby Carnival glass (1991).

These items were made by Fenton for QVC (in Fenton's system, all QVC ware numbers are preceded by the letter "C").

947. C5858 NZ 8" cornshock vase, Shell Pink with Salem Blue crest and handpainted blue floral (1990).

948. C7562 JQ bell, Milk Glass with Ruby crest, handpainted red poinsettia (1988).

949. C4661 RB Burmese 5½" pitcher with handpainted roses (1991).

950. C7244 QX Rosalene 8½" basket with handpainted roses (1991).

951. C7580 EQ Dolphin candy dish, Shell Pink with handpainted blue floral (1990).

952. C7668 XA Christmas bell, blue border and church motif handpainted on Opal Carnival glass (1990).

953. C7668 XA Christmas bell, green border and church motif handpainted on Opal Carnival glass (1990).

954. C7668 UW bell, Thanksgiving motif handpainted on Shell Pink satin (1990).

955. C7668 XA bell, Christmas motif with handpainted roses and pine on Opal Carnival glass (1990).

956. C1773 UQ bell, Mother's Day, handpainted lamb on Opal Satin (1989).

957. C7668 MN bell, Mother's Day, handpainted baby birds on Opal Satin (1990).

958. C7668 VD bell, Valentine's Day, handpainted ribbons and floral with porcelain rose, on iridized Opal (1990).

959. C7668 QC Christmas musical bell, church motif and Lord's prayer on Opal Satin (1988).

960. C5165 XT cat, handpainted floral on Opal Satin (1990).

961. C5151 W10 Birthstone Bear (sold during several years).

962. C5151 XT bear, handpainted floral on Opal Satin (1990).

963-967. C8691 EQ clock, C7662 EQ petite bell, C7667 EQ bell, C5165 EQ cat, and C5161 EQ swan, Shell Pink with handpainted blue floral (1988).

153

Unless otherwise indicated, these special items were made by Fenton for glass collectors' clubs or other organizations.

968. Cobalt Carnival ruffled and crimped bowl, with Lions interior and Fenton Flowers exterior (International Carnival Glass Association, 1984).

969. Ruby Carnival 3-toed rolled edge bowl, Butterfly & Berry exterior, Good Luck Horseshoe logo and hand-painted decoration (Heart of America Carnival Glass Association, 1984).

970. Sample Marigold Opalescent Carnival glass bowl, Fenton Flowers exterior, plain interior.

971. Cobalt Carnival glass 3-toed bowl, Lions interior and Fenton Flowers exterior (International Carnival Glass Association, 1984).

972. Ruby Carnival bell, Harry Northwood portrait and Good Luck Horseshoe logo (Heart of America Carnival Glass Association, 1985).

973. Holiday Green Carnival pitcher with handpainted violets (International Carnival Glass Association, 1987).

974. Marigold Carnival bell, Edward Muhleman-Imperial Glass Co. and Good Luck Horseshoe logo (Heart of America Carnival Glass Association, 1988).

975. Holiday Green Carnival Valencia candy dish with hand-painted lid (International Carnival Glass Association, 1990).

976. Cobalt Carnival Fisherman's pitcher (Pacific Northwest Carnival Glass Association, 1984).

977. Green Carnival hatpin holder (Heart of America Carnival Glass Association, 1980).

978. Green Carnival Basketweave cuspidor (Canadian Carnival Glass Association, 1985).

979. Ruby Carnival paperweight with embossed town pump logo (International Carnival Glass Association, 1983).

980. Light Blue Carnival Corn vase with Good Luck Horseshoe logo (Heart of America Carnival Glass Association, 1982).

981. Cobalt Carnival coaster (Australian Carnival Glass Enthusiasts, 1985).

982. Teal Carnival Fisherman's mug (Pacific Northwest Carnival Glass Association, 1988).

983. Teal Green Carnival Seacoast cuspidor (American Carnival Glass Association, 1985).

(cont'd. top of next page)

(cont'd. from previous page)

984. Marigold Carnival miniature Town Pump (International Carnival Glass Association, 1980)

985. French Opalescent Elephant (Heisey Collectors of America, 1988).

986. Blue Burmese Melon vase with peloton treatment (Fenton Art Glass Collectors of America, 1984).

987-988. Bermuda Red Carnival God and Home miniature pitcher and tumblers (Dorothy Taylor's Encore, 1981).

989. French Opalescent Elephant (Heisey Collectors of America, 1988).

990. Topaz Opalescent Carnival miniature mug (Heart of America Carnival Glass Association, 1981).

991. Marigold Carnival Seacoast cuspidor (American Carnival Glass Association, 1982).

992. Rosalene Oscar or Plug Horse (Heisey Collectors of America, 1990).

These special items and souvenirs were made by Fenton for the Fenton Art Glass Collectors of America, Inc., as noted.

993. Amethyst with white hanging hearts vase (1981).

994. Jade Opaline Melon basket with Holiday Green crest and handle (1990)

995. Dusty Rose Overlay Melon vase with mica flecks (1985).

996. Dusty Rose Overlay tulip vase with Peachblow interior and cobalt blue crest (1987).

997. Cobalt Blue Overlay Melon vase with mica flecks (1985)

998. Cranberry Opalescent 1-pc. fairy light (1983).

999. Cobalt Vasa Murrhina vase (1979).

1000. Ruby iridized art glass vase (1986).

1001. Blue Burmese Melon vase with peloton treatment (1984).

1002. Rose overlay Melon vase with bubble optic (1980).

1003. Ruby Carnival butterfly (1989).

1004. Burmese mug (1985).

1005. Chocolate oval Fenton logo sign (1982).

These Aqua Opal Carnival (IO) items were made by Fenton for Levay in 1980.

1006. 3407 IO 7-pc. Cactus water set (pitcher and 6 goblets).

1007. 2805 IO Wild Rose and Bowknot 20" student lamp.

These Purple Stretch (VY) items were made for Levay in 1981.

1008. 7551 VY 6" Dolphin fan vase.

1009. 8435 VY Diamond & Thread pie crust crimped 9" basket (also shown with flowers).

1010. 7505 VY 5-pc. star crimped epergne.

1011. 7509 VY 7-pc. tankard water set.

1012. 8455 VY Diamond & Thread double crimped 7" vase.

1013. 7563 VY star crimped bell.

1014. 7590 VY toothpick holder.

1015. 7567 VY miniature basket.

1016. 5153 VY miniature vase in hand.

1017. 7581 VY Dolphin loving cup.

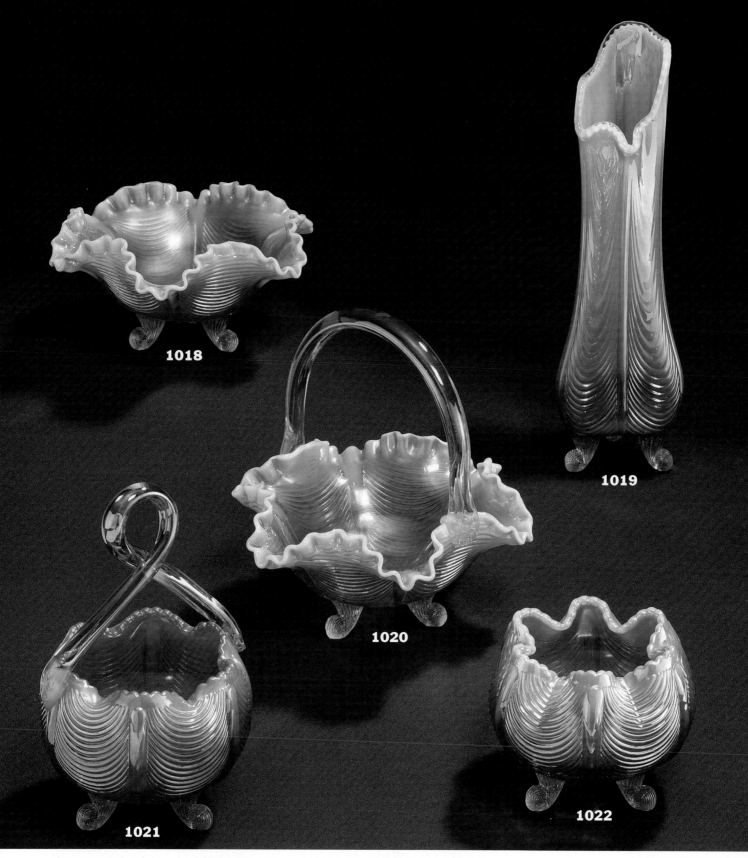

1018

1019

1020

1021

1022

These Aqua Opal Carnival (IO) items were made by Fenton for Levay in 1980. These same shapes (except for the 9456 swung vase) were made in iridized Plum Opalescent (IP) in mid-1984, and all were made in iridized Green Opalescent in late 1984 (this treatment was described as "butterscotch" green opalescent, suggesting that a marigold spray was used).

1018. 9425 IO ribbon candy edge 8" bowl.

1019. 9456 IO 12" swung vase.

1020. 9435 IO ribbon candy edge 8½" basket.

1021. 9436 IO 8½" rose bowl basket with looped handle.

1022. 8454 IO 5" rose bowl.

These Red Sunset Carnival (RN) items in the Cactus pattern were made for Levay in 1982.

1023. 3436 RN 7½" double-crimped basket with ribbed looped handle.

1024. 3463 RN cruet.

1025. 3495 RN toothpick.

1026. 3433 RN 10" double crimped basket.

1027. 3407 RN 7-pc. water set.

1028-1029. 3408 RN covered sugar and creamer set.

1030. 3480 RN covered cracker jar.

1031. 3429 RN footed double crimped compote.

1032. 3432 RN single crimped pie crust banana basket with ribbed looped handle.

1033. 3431 RN 10" double crimped cracker basket.

1034. 3434 RN 10" basket vase.

1035. 3426 RN ladies' cuspidor.

1036. 3427 RN gentleman's cuspidor.

1037. 3441 RN double crimped jack in the pulpit vase.

1038. 3483 RN 9" swung vase.

158

These Pink Opalescent (UO) Hobnail items were part of Fenton's Collectors Extravaganza offering in 1988 (ware numbers are preceded by the letter "A" in Fenton's records).

1039. A3712 UO 14-pc. master punch set (bowl on stand with 12 cups).

1040. A3908 UO 7-pc. water set.

1041. A3701 UO 10" jack-in-the-pulpit epergne.

1042. A3720 UO 12" pie crust crimped banana stand.

1043. A3854 UO 4¹/₂" ruffled top rose bowl.

1044. A3795 UO toothpick.

1045. A3834 UO basket.

1046. A3861 UO crimped rose bowl.

1047. A3863 UO cruet with stopper.

159

These miniature items were made by Fenton for Doris Lechler's Heirlooms of Tomorrow collection.

1048. Custard ruffled lemonade pitcher with six tumblers.

1049. Custard tumble up set.

1050. Custard tumble up set with handpainted violets.

1051. Custard pitcher and six tumblers with handpainted violets and tray.

1052. Ruby overlay tumble up set (decanter and tumbler).

1053. Amethyst ruffled pitcher and six tumblers with handpainted lily of the valley decoration and tray.

1054. Custard ruffled pitcher and six tumblers with handpainted Christmas Holly decoration and tray.

1055. Burmese ruffled pitcher and six tumblers with handpainted roses.

These Peach Opalescent Carnival glass (PI) Atlantis pattern items were made for MLT Glass in 1981.

1056. 5150 PI hi bowl A.   **1057.** 5150 PI vase B.   **1058.** 5150 PI spittoon C.

DESCRIPTIONS OF COVERS

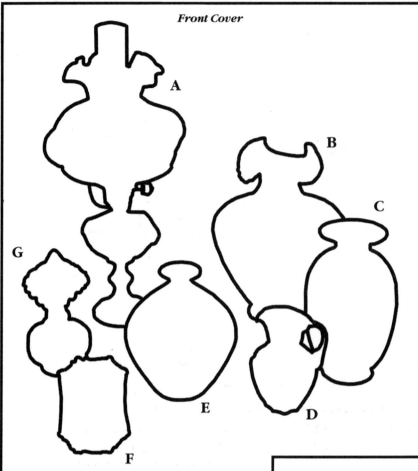

Front Cover

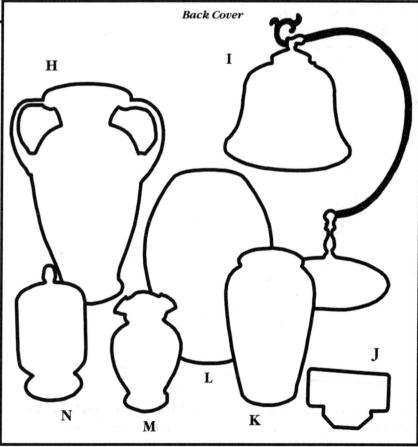

Back Cover

A. Connoisseur Collection (1989) Rosalene Satin 9308 TT lamp with handpainted decoration.

B. Country Cranberry Coin Dot Optic 1443 CC 10¹/₂" vase 1990-91).

C. Azure Blue Satin vase (made for Avon's Gallery Originals in 1984).

D. C1866 XN Fern pitcher, Ocean Blue Opalescent with Cobalt Blue crest and handle (made for QVC in 1990).

E. Connoisseur Collection (1985) Burmese 8808 SB vase with hand-painted decoration.

F. 9555 EO Minted Cream votive (1986).

G. Connoisseur Collection (1988) cased French Opalescent and ruby with teal crest iridized 2556 ZI 6" tulip vase.

H. Connoisseur Collection (1986) French Cranberry 3194 ZS 13" handled urn.

I. Wisteria Lane 9702 JW lamp (1986).

J. Rosalene Fenton logo.

K. Connoisseur Collection (1983) Sculptured Rose Quartz 7661 LJ 9" Lady vase.

L. 8802 LY Gabrielle sandcarved 12" oval vase (Connoisseur Collection, 1985).

M. Wildflowers 7530 FD 6¹/₂" vase (1983).

N. Teal Marigold 9480 OI Chessie candy box (1990).

Chapter Twenty-Seven
SOUVENIRS

During the 1980s, Fenton made numerous special order souvenirs for various organizations. Listing all of them would be beyond the scope of this book and, perhaps, beyond all possibility, as Fenton's own records are sometimes rather sketchy. These souvenirs are typically marked with the club's name or logo as well as the year. Frank M. Fenton was almost always involved with the souvenir pieces for glass collectors' clubs, and the company's records contain many memos "for the record" in which Frank summarized his discussions with representatives of a club. He typically quoted a per-piece wholesale price based upon the quantity and the anticipated difficulty of production. He also provided assistance when club members sought advice about mouldmaking or needed alterations to a mould (or part of a mould such as a bottom plate which had a date).

In addition to the souvenirs (which were sold by the clubs to members for a set price), Fenton usually made a small number of "whimsies" from whatever mould was in production for the souvenir piece. These whimsies were bought by the club and re-sold to members, typically at an auction following the convention banquet. Bidding was often quite spirited, and prices in three figures were not uncommon. The auction provided a nice profit for the club's treasury, as Frank generally set prices for whimsies at a modest surcharge over the regular souvenir.

Club officers or those in charge of the souvenirs sometimes came to Fenton when the pieces were in production. Such visits occasionally afforded insights into the daily frustrations of glassmaking. Roland Kuhn, representing the Heart of America Carnival Glass Association, came to Williamstown in early February, 1983, to spend two days at the factory.

The first day's work at Fenton produced only about 100 good pieces, far less than the 300 anticipated. Things went better the next day, however, and Kuhn was relieved when the souvenirs were completed. Grace and Byron Rinehart arrived in the middle of the second day, and they came to appreciate the problems, too: "It is a very revealing experience to see the time and work that it takes to get the souvenirs made. We feet it a privilege every time, and the souvenirs seem to mean more to us when we have had a chance to see all the different steps it takes from beginning to the end—then they finally end up on our shelves as a treasured memento" (Heart of America Carnival Glass Association newsletter, March, 1983).

Fenton made the "Seacoast" cuspidor in several different colors for the American Carnival Glass Association (ACGA) in the early and mid-1980s. These were made in Peach Opalescent Carnival glass (1982), Meadow Green with marigold iridescence (1983), Ruby Carnival glass (1984), and Teal Blue Carnival glass (1985).

Fenton's association with the Heart of America Carnival Glass Association (HOACGA) goes back to the 1970s, when a whiskey decanter and shot glasses were made. Like the other HOACGA souvenirs, these have the "Good Luck" horseshoe logo. In 1980, a hatpin holder was produced in Ice Green Carnival glass, and a two-piece Red Carnival Grape and Cable candle lamp was made in 1981. A facsimile of the Northwood Corn Vase in Ice Blue Carnival glass appeared 1n 1982, and a replica of Fenton's Loving Cup in custard glass with marigold iridescence was made in 1983 (this had been made in Red Carnival glass in 1979). Another old Fenton motif, Butterfly and Berry, was used for the 1984 souvenir, a Ruby Carnival 3-toed bowl.

In 1985, HOACGA issued the first in a series of bells which commemorated five pioneers in American glassmaking who were associated with iridescent ware during the 1908-1915 heyday of this now highly collectible glass. The first bell, in Red Carnival glass, featured Harry Northwood, who founded H. Northwood and Co. at Wheeling in 1902.

The next two bells (Green Opalescent Carnival glass in 1986 and Cobalt Blue Carnival glass in 1987, respectively) honored Frank L. Fenton and John W. Fenton. These men founded the Fenton Art Glass Company at Martins Ferry, Ohio, in 1905, and they built the Williamstown factory in 1906. John W. Fenton was also associated with the Millersburg Glass Company (and its successor, the Radium Glass Company) from 1909-1912.

The 1988 Marigold Carnival glass bell featured Edward Muhleman, who was involved with the Elson Glass Company in Martins Ferry in the 1880s and helped to form two Bellaire-based organizations, the Crystal Glass Company and the Imperial Glass Company. The Imperial firm made Carnival glass beginning about 1908 or 1909. Thomas E. A. Dugan was depicted on the 1989

This Fenton Loving Cup was made in custard glass with marigold iridescense for HOACGA in 1983.

presents its 1986 Souvenir

The FAGCA's Butterfly Net mug was made in Rosalene for the 1986 convention.

Teal Blue Carnival bell. He was an integral part of the Dugan Glass Company in Indiana, Pa., from 1904 to 1913.

The historical connections among the five men commemorated by HOACGA are really quite remarkable. Harry Northwood and his cousin Thomas E. A. Dugan emigrated from England and worked together in Martins Ferry (1888-1893), Ellwood City, Pa. (1893-1896), and Indiana, Pa. (1896-1899). Frank L. Fenton began his career as a decorator in the Indiana plant in 1897, and both he and his brother John W. Fenton probably worked at Northwood's Wheeling plant in 1903-04. Muhleman and Northwood were neighbors on Wheeling Island.

The International Carnival Glass Association (ICGA) had Fenton make its Frolicking Bears cuspidor in several colors: Aqua Opal Carnival glass (1981), Ruby Carnival glass (1982) and Custard with Marigold iridescence (1983). The souvenir for 1984 was a Cobalt Carnival glass bowl with Lions interior and Fenton Flowers exterior), and the same bowl was made in Marigold Carnival for 1985. In 1986, the ICGA souvenir was a Poppy rose bowl in iridized green opalescent

In 1987, Frank Fenton and decorator Linda Everson went to the ICGA convention. Arrangements were made so that Linda could demonstrate her skills, and ICGA members could order custom-decorated pitchers. The completed pitchers, which featured various floral motifs and personalized messages, had to be taken back to the factory to be fired before being shipped to the individual customers.

The 1988 ICGA souvenir was a Topaz Opalescent basket, and the 1989 souvenir was a Flute-Dot vase. In 1990, Fenton made Hunter Green iridized Valencia comports which were then given handpainted decorations.

Among the other Carnival glass collectors' clubs which commissioned Fenton to make souvenirs for one or more occasions during the 1980s were the Lincoln-Land Carnival Glass Club, the Pacific Northwest Carnival Glass Club, the Australian Carnival Glass Enthusiasts, and the Canadian Carnival Glass Association. Fenton also produced souvenirs for other glass collector's clubs, such as the Heisey Collectors of America and the National Duncan Glass Society.

As this is being written in mid-1996, the Fenton Art Glass Company is doing very well, indeed. Fenton products are well known nationwide, and the company is at the forefront of the hand glass industry. Fenton glass is the choice of many customers, ranging from the avid collector to the casual giftware purchaser. The firm now employs over 500 people, the largest figure in its 90-year history.

The survival of the Fenton Art Glass Company during the difficult decade of the 1980s was no fluke. Prudent management had anticipated and prepared for the tough times, and, when needed, innovative approaches and hard work combined to regain Fenton's traditional position in giftware outlets and to open new markets as well. The strength of the Fenton Art Glass Company's relationships with its sales reps and its employees served the company well.

The Fenton Art Glass Company continues to learn from both its successes and its shortcomings. The entire Fenton family—management, employees and sales reps—is strongly committed to programs which encourage cooperation and unity of effort to enhance efficiency and quality.

With its centennial now less than a decade away, the Fenton Art Glass Company looks forward to continued success as it foresees both challenges and changes. The future is bright.

CORRECTIONS TO EARLIER FENTON BOOKS

ADDITIONS AND CORRECTIONS TO *FENTON GLASS: THE FIRST TWENTY-FIVE YEARS.*

p. 15. Imperial and Dugan-Diamond made red Carnival glass; Northwood apparently did not.

pp. 16-21. Further research has identified the manufacturers of some of these patterns:

Carolina Dogwood (p. 17) was made by Westmoreland.

Cosmos Variant (p. 18) was made by Dugan-Diamond.

Floral & Grape, Flowers & Frames, and Flowers and Spades (all on p. 19) were made by Dugan-Diamond.

Four Flowers (p. 20), Grapevine Lattice (p. 20) and Lattice and Daisy (p. 21) were all made by Dugan-Diamond.

p. 17. Add the Fenton pattern Cherry Chain Variant (Hartung 5-61)—which was made in plates, bowls and bon bons—and is illustrated on p. 57.

p. 18. Elk Bells were also made for the Parkersburg and the Portland, Oregon, conventions.

p. 19. The Fenton rib vase is often called "Fine Rib." Also, add the Fenton pattern Floral and Grape Variant and see the pitcher and tumbler illustrated on p. 81.

p. 25. The Dancing Ladies urn is *possibly* Northwood's satin-finished ivory glass, c. 1917-19. Fenton's vaseline opalescent and amethyst opalescent Carnival glass are *possibly* (but not undoubtedly!) experimental colors.

p. 29. Jacob Rosenthal was not related to the Fenton family.

p. 31, figs. 47-50. Honeycomb <u>and</u> Clover, not Honeycomb <u>with</u> Clover.

p. 32, fig. 56. This Lattice and Daisy tumbler is a Dugan-Diamond product.

p. 37, figs. 123-124. The mould number for Apple Tree is 1561.

p. 38, figs. 136-137. The mould number for Cherries & Blossoms is 821.

p. 41. Insert a caption for figs. 163-164, Fenton's Wine and Roses wine glass and pitcher; delete the reference to figs. 172-173, which are on the next page.

p. 49, fig. 214. Water Lily is number 1804.

p. 57, fig. 297. This pattern is Cherry Chain Variant.

p. 58, fig. 305. Now known to be a Dugan-Diamond product.

p. 59, fig. 312. This is probably a Dugan-Diamond product rather than Northwood.

p. 61, fig. 323. These pieces are Celeste Blue, not Wisteria.

p. 64, fig. 362. This is probably Northwood's No. 707 bowl, which goes under its No. 706 ash tray; for the Fenton footed fern dish, see p. 86.

p. 66, fig. 388. This is Northwood's No. 707 bulb bowl.

p. 69, fig. 418. This is Fenton's No. 1608, not No. 160.

p. 70, fig. 437. Definitely Fenton, but not as rare as first thought!

p. 73. These pieces are "Grecian Gold" rather than Marigold.

p. 75, fig. 490. Coasters, not casters!

p. 77, fig. 509. Made in plain green c. 1929, the Turtle is also known in amber.

p. 118, Group K. These circa 1915 products are Dugan-Diamond, not Fenton.

p. 122, fig. C. This is a Dugan-Diamond product, not Fenton.

ADDITIONS AND CORRECTIONS TO *FENTON GLASS: THE SECOND TWENTY-FIVE YEARS.*

p. 8. The sketch at lower left depicts Fenton's Dancing Ladies covered bon bon or candy jar.

p. 25, figs. 1 and 3. The numbers in parentheses are "ware numbers" instituted in July, 1952. Before that, Fenton used either mould numbers or pattern numbers.

p. 25, figs. 2, 4 and 5. This color was originally called Satin Rose, and the name was later changed to Rose Satin (today's collectors call the color "Cranberry Opalescent Satin").

p. 26. Although most of Northwood's Chinese Coral is red-orange, some pieces are indeed similar to Fenton's "Flame." See the illustrations in Heacock, Measell and Wiggins' *Harry Northwood: The Wheeling Years, 1901-1925*, especially pp. 141-142.

p. 59, figs. 476-477. Beaded Melon was No. 711.

p. 59, figs. 482 and 484. These items were made by both Fenton and McKee, and research continues on the similarity of these pieces.

p. 59, fig. 485. Not Fenton, this atomizer was probably made by Duncan Miller for the T. J. Holmes Co.

p. 61, fig. 510. This is the No. 4303 Lamb's Tongue mayonnaise.

p. 63, fig. 536. This vase was called Sung Ko.

ADDITIONS AND CORRECTIONS TO *FENTON GLASS: THE THIRD TWENTY-FIVE YEARS.*

p. 88, fig. 408. Not Fenton! This piece was made by the Imperial Glass Corporation of Bellaire, Ohio.

INDEX